FUGITIVES' REUNION

VANDERBILT STUDIES IN THE HUMANITIES

VOLUME III

William Elliott   Merrill Moore   Jesse Wills   Sidney Hirsch
Alfred Starr   Alec Stevenson   Robert Penn Warren
Allen Tate   John Crowe Ransom   Donald Davidson

This photograph of the assembled Fugitives was made during the noontime recess between the morning and afternoon sessions of Friday, May 4, which were held at the home of Mr. and Mrs. Wills, on Belle Meade Boulevard.

FUGITIVES' REUNION

Conversations at Vanderbilt

May 3-5, 1956

Edited by ROB ROY PURDY

Introduction by LOUIS D. RUBIN, JR.

VANDERBILT UNIVERSITY PRESS

Nashville

EDITOR'S PREFACE

THE reunion of the Fugitives, some thirty years after the discontinuance of their magazine, was made possible by a grant from the Rockefeller Foundation to the American Studies Association, whose secretary, Louis D. Rubin, Jr., had originated the proposal. Fortunately the occasion came no later than it did, for within a year three of the active participants —Alfred Starr, Merrill Moore, and Frank Owsley—had died.

The meetings were of two types, open and closed, and there were also two dinners to which wives and friends were invited. The first meeting, on the afternoon of Thursday, May 3, 1956, was held in Neely Auditorium, and was open to the public. After remarks by Andrew Lytle, Allen Tate, and Robert Penn Warren, the meeting adjourned to Alumni Hall for an exhibition of Fugitive writings and memorabilia prepared by Mrs. Brainard Cheney and Miss Isabel Howell. The dinner meeting on that evening, in Rand Hall, had as its toastmaster Alec Stevenson, and as speakers, Alfred Starr, Jesse Wills, and Donald Davidson. At the Friday dinner meeting, which was held at the Belle Meade Country Club, the members of the group with their wives were the guests of Harold Vanderbilt, President of the Vanderbilt University Board of Trust, and Mrs. Vanderbilt. The host presided at the program, which included talks by Chancellor Harvie Branscomb, Robert Selph Henry (who spoke as a member of the Board of Trust and a contemporary of the Fugitive group), and John Crowe Ransom. The dinner was followed by a public reading of their own poems—to an overflow crowd in Neely Auditorium—

by Robert Penn Warren, Merrill Moore, Allen Tate, Donald Davidson, and John Crowe Ransom. The readings were preceded by a historical account of the Fugitive movement, by William Yandell Elliott.

For reasons of space, this volume does not include the remarks made at the public and semi-public gatherings. Its text is of the closed sessions only, the real meat of the conference. These were four in number. The first was held on Thursday evening in Randall Stewart's apartment on Elliston Place. The discussion was touched off by some remarks Donald Davidson had made at the Thursday evening dinner, on the limitations of modern poetry, on the need for poetry to divorce itself from the book and to reassert its former oral character. From here the conversation ranged over a wide variety of topics, continuing through the second and third sessions on Friday morning and afternoon (these were held at Jesse Wills's home on Belle Meade Boulevard, where the members were entertained at lunch by Mr. and Mrs. Wills), and culminating in the fourth session, at Alumni Hall, where the talk reached a climax in the probing analysis of the relations between the Fugitive and Agrarian movements. Despite the wide range of subjects discussed, the four sessions have a unity of their own, a continuum that becomes apparent by reading the sections of the text in order. A final luncheon meeting on Saturday, in Rand Hall, provided the group some summary comments by Cleanth Brooks and others. Parts of these have been included in this volume.

Participating in the closed sessions were ten critics and observers who were invited to attend, some because they had made a special study of the Fugitives and their work, some because as contemporaries they could join in the reminiscing about *Fugitive* days.

All the proceedings were tape-recorded. The editorial aim in this volume is to let the document show just what was said, how it was said, and in what context. To preserve the conversational tone, the text reproduces the language of informal talk; there are occasional anacolutha, fragmentary sentences, repetitions. To aid the reader further in experiencing a sense of being actually present, there have been added parenthetical descriptive helps to indicate the group response to what is being said. Footnotes have been used only where it was felt necessary to identify references of a particularly local nature.

Grateful acknowledgment is made to Mr. Rubin, to the American Studies Association, and to the Rockefeller Foundation—in particular to John Marshall—for making the Fugitives' Reunion possible; to Vanderbilt University, Chancellor Branscomb, and Mr. Vanderbilt for acting as hosts to the conference; to the Vanderbilt Committee on the Humanities and its chairman, Lloyd Stow, for providing funds for the publication of this volume; to Randall Stewart, Richmond Beatty, Charles Bledsoe, and Robert McGaw for editorial assistance in the preparation of the text. Special acknowledgment is due Professor Stewart, whose guiding genius was largely responsible not only for bringing the group together, but also for the successful staging of the conference and for the preparation and completion of this volume.

Rob Roy Purdy

Vanderbilt University
March, 1959.

CONTENTS

PARTICIPANTS

Fugitives

DONALD DAVIDSON
  b. Campbellsville, Tenn., 1893. B.A. Vanderbilt, 1917; M.A., 1922. Member of the Vanderbilt English department since 1920. Literary editor, *Nashville Tennessean*, 1924-30. Faculty, Bread Loaf School of English since 1931. Author: *Lee in the Mountains*, 1938; *The Attack on Leviathan*, 1938; *The Tennessee* (1946-1948) ; *Still Rebels, Still Yankees*, 1957; and others.

WILLIAM Y. ELLIOTT
  b. Murfreesboro, Tenn., 1896. B.A. Vanderbilt, 1917; M.A., 1920. Rhodes Scholar 1921-23, Balliol College; Ph.D. Oxford, 1923. Instructor in English, Vanderbilt, 1919-20; Member of the Department of Government, University of California, 1923-25, and at Harvard since 1925. Author: *The Pragmatic Revolt in Politics*, 1928; *Political Economy of the Foreign Policy of the United States*, 1955; and other books in political science.

SIDNEY HIRSCH
  b. Nashville, Tenn., 1885. Educated in the Nashville city schools. After several years in the Navy, was associated with the James L. Frazer Company in New York. Author: *The Fire Regained* (a Greek pageant produced in Nashville and in Washington, D. C.) , *The Passion Play of Washington Square*, and other dramatic works.

MERRILL MOORE
  b. Columbia, Tenn., 1903. d. 1957. B.A. Vanderbilt, 1924; M.D., 1928. Clinical associate at Harvard Medical School and practicing psychiatrist in Boston. Author of some 100,000 sonnets and several books of poems including *The Noise That Time Makes*, 1929; *M:*

11

One Thousand Autobiographical Sonnets, 1938; *Clinical Sonnets,* 1950; and other volumes of poetry.

JOHN CROWE RANSOM
b. Pulaski, Tenn., 1888. B.A. Vanderbilt, 1909; Rhodes Scholar, 1910-13, Christ Church College; B.A. (Lit. Hum.) Oxford, 1913. Vanderbilt English department, 1914-37; Carnegie Professor of Poetry at Kenyon College, 1937-58. Editor of *The Kenyon Review,* 1939-58. Author: *Poems About God,* 1919; *Chills and Fever,* 1924; *Two Gentlemen in Bonds,* 1926; *God Without Thunder,* 1930; *The World's Body,* 1938; *The New Criticism,* 1941; *Selected Poems,* 1945.

ALFRED STARR
b. Nashville, Tenn., 1898. d. 1957. Vanderbilt, 1922-24; B.A. Harvard, 1926. President Bijou theater chain. President of Theater Owners of America, 1952. One of the founders of the Nashville Symphony Association and the Nashville Arts Council.

ALEC B. STEVENSON
b. Toronto, Canada, 1895. B.A. Vanderbilt, 1916. Investment banker in Nashville, resident partner Vance, Sanders and Company. Author of several books and articles on financial subjects including *Shares in Mutual Investment Funds.* Member of the Vanderbilt Board of Trust.

ALLEN TATE
b. Clarke County, Ky., 1899. B.A. Vanderbilt, 1922. Teaching positions at Southwestern at Memphis, Princeton, New York University, University of Chicago, Woman's College of the University of North Carolina, and at University of Minnesota (since 1951). Chair of Poetry, Library of Congress, 1943-44. Editor, *The Sewanee Review,* 1944-46. Author: *Stonewall Jackson,* 1928; *Mr. Pope and Other Poems,* 1928; *Jefferson Davis,* 1929; *Mediterranean and Other Poems,* 1936; *Reactionary Essays,* 1936; *Selected Poems,* 1937; *The Fathers,* 1938; *Reason in Madness,* 1941; *Poems, 1922-1947,* 1948; *Forlorn Demon,* 1952.

ROBERT PENN WARREN
b. Guthrie, Ky., 1905. B.A. Vanderbilt, 1925; M.A. University of California, 1927; Student at Yale, 1927-28; Rhodes Scholar, B. Litt., Oxford, 1930. Teaching positions: Southwestern at Memphis, 1930-31; Vanderbilt, 1931-34; Louisiana State University, 1934-36; University of Minnesota, 1942-50; Yale University, 1950-55. Co-editor (with Cleanth Brooks), *The Southern Review,* 1935-42. Chair of

Poetry, Library of Congress, 1944-45. Author: *John Brown,* 1929; *Thirty-Six Poems,* 1936; *Night Rider,* 1939; *Eleven Poems on the Same Theme,* 1942; *At Heaven's Gate,* 1943; *Selected Poems,* 1944; *All the King's Men,* 1946 (Pulitzer Prize); *Circus in the Attic and Other Stories,* 1947; *World Enough and Time,* 1950; *Brother to Dragons,* 1953; *Band of Angels,* 1955; *Promises,* 1958 (Pulitzer Prize); *Collected Essays,* 1958.

JESSE WILLS
b. Nashville, Tenn., 1899. B.A. Vanderbilt, 1922. With the National Life and Accident Insurance Company since 1922; executive vice-president since 1953. Author: *Early & Late: Fugitive Poems and Others,* 1959. Member of the Vanderbilt Board of Trust.

Others

RICHMOND CROOM BEATTY
b. Shawnee, Okla., 1905. B.A. Birmingham Southern College, 1926, M.A. Vanderbilt, 1928, Ph.D., 1930. Taught at Memphis State College and the University of Alabama; member of Vanderbilt English department 1937-1957. Literary editor *The Nashville Tennessean* since 1957. Author: *William Byrd of Westover,* 1932; *Bayard Taylor,* 1936; *Lord Macaulay,* 1938; *James Russell Lowell,* 1942; Editor: *A Vanderbilt Miscellany,* 1944; and other works.

DOROTHY BETHURUM
b. Franklin, Tenn., 1897; B.A. Vanderbilt, 1919, M.A., 1922; Ph.D. Yale, 1930. Taught at Randolph-Macon College for Women, Lawrence College, and Connecticut College (since 1940). Author: *The Homilies of Wulfstan,* 1957.

CLEANTH BROOKS
b. Murray, Ky., 1908. B.A. Vanderbilt, 1928, M.A. Tulane, 1929. Rhodes Scholar, 1929-32; B.A. (honors) Oxford, 1931; B. Litt., 1932. Member English Department Louisiana State University, and Yale (since 1947). Co-editor (with Robert Penn Warren), *The Southern Review,* 1935-42. Author: *Modern Poetry and the Tradition,* 1939, and *The Well Wrought Urn,* 1947.

WILLIAM COBB
b. Nashville, Tenn., 1902. B.A. Vanderbilt, 1922; M.A., 1923. College editor, Houghton-Mifflin Company. Editor of Publications with the Rockefeller Foundation (since 1953).

LOUISE COWAN

b. Fort Worth, Texas, 1916. B.A. Texas Christian University, 1946; M.A., 1947; Ph.D. Vanderbilt, 1953. Member English Department, Texas Christian University, since 1954. Author: *The Fugitive Group: A Literary History*, a forthcoming volume to be published by the Louisiana State University Press.

ROBERT JACOBS

b. Vicksburg, Miss., 1918. B.A. University of Mississippi; Ph.D. Johns Hopkins University. Member of English Department, Johns Hopkins University, University of Kentucky (since 1953). Co-editor (with Louis Rubin) of *The Hopkins Review*, and *Southern Renascence* (1953). Contributor to numerous magazines and periodicals.

ANDREW LYTLE

b. Murfreesboro, Tenn., 1902. B.A. Vanderbilt, 1925; Student, Yale School of Drama, 1927-28. Taught at University of the South, and University of Florida (since 1948); Editor, *The Sewanee Review*, 1942-43. Author: *Bedford Forest and His Critter Company*, 1931; *The Long Night*, 1936; *A Name for Evil*, 1936; *The Velvet Horn*, 1957.

FRANK OWSLEY

b. Montgomery County, Ala., 1890; d. 1957. B.S. Alabama Polytechnic Institute, 1911; M.S., 1912; M.A. University of Chicago, 1917; Ph.D., 1924. Member of History Department, Vanderbilt, 1920-49; University of Alabama, 1949-57. Author: *States Rights in the Confederacy*, 1925; *King Cotton Diplomacy*, 1931; *Plain Folk of the Old South*, 1949.

LOUIS RUBIN

b. Charleston, S.C., 1923; B.A. University of Richmond; Ph.D. Johns Hopkins. Secretary of American Studies' Association, 1953-56. Chairman, English Department, Hollins College. Co-editor (with Robert Jacobs) of *The Hopkins Review*, and *Southern Renascence* (1953). Author: *Thomas Wolfe: the Weather of His Youth*, 1955.

WILLARD THORP

b. Sidney, N.Y., 1899. B.A. Hamilton College, 1920; M.A. Harvard, 1921; Ph.D. Princeton, 1926. Member Princeton English Department since 1926. Author: *The Triumph of Realism in Elizabethan Drama*, 1928; Editor: *Herman Melville, Representative Selections*, 1938; and *A Southern Reader*, 1955.

INTRODUCTION

by Louis D. Rubin, Jr.

Iɴ April of the year 1922, there was published in the city of
Nashville, Tennessee, a little magazine of poetry, bearing
the title of *The Fugitive,* and containing verse by such oddly-
christened poets as Roger Prim, Henry Feathertop, Robin
Gallivant, Dendric, and other improbable names. It was a
time of much issuing of little magazines, and *The Fugitive*
was much like other little magazines of the day: there were
poems, there was a manifesto, and a knowing air about it all.

Unlike most of the little magazines of the day, however,
The Fugitive's verse had very little of the precious or the
pretentious about it. For one thing, the poetry tended to be
rather formal, even a bit caustic. During a time of considerable
caprice and striking of attitudes in verse, the poetry of *The
Fugitive* was characterized for the most part by a serious and
hard-wrought dignity. Above all, it had what was lacking in
most little magazine verse, a genuine feeling for form. It was
small wonder, then, that *The Fugitive* received praise and attention on a national scale, such as the first issues of most little
poetry magazines do not customarily get. Small wonder, too,
that the names of some of the contributors to *The Fugitive,*
their pseudonyms abandoned after the second number, subsequently became among the best known and most important
in twentieth-century letters. For that group of young men who
formed a poetry association and in 1922 began issuing their
magazine included John Crowe Ransom, Allen Tate, Donald

15

Davidson, Merrill Moore, and, a bit later, Robert Penn Warren.

It was a luminous group; there is no other word for it. Nor was its brilliance confined to those five. There were others whose later intellectual achievement would lie outside the field of the writing of poetry—Walter Clyde Curry, the English literature scholar, and William Yandell Elliott, the political theorist. There were some who became businessmen, with marked success, and whose lives continued afterward to be enriched by their youthful literary endeavors. Finally, there were still others whose later careers for various reasons did not seem to bear out the literary promise of those earlier years, but who during the days of *The Fugitive* were among the most active of participants. What is astonishing about the entire Fugitive group is the striking degree of success attained by almost all the members in their chosen occupations, whether the creation of literature, the practice of criticism and scholarship, the management of business, or the practice of other professions. In whatever they chose to do, almost all of the Nashville Fugitives "made good."

Because of the reputation enjoyed nowadays by the men who constituted the Nashville Fugitives, there is considerable interest in the group among students of twentieth century America letters. Nor is it simply the presence of a surprisingly large number of important poets and novelists in the group that occasions this interest; it is something much rarer even than that. For the Nashville Fugitives were not simply an array of promising young poets; they were a *group*, a functioning organization, a dynamic unit of young men who performed their literary labors in common and who cooperated with each other in the perfecting of their art. There is, on the part of those who have studied the Fugitives, the definite conviction that the group identity contributed importantly, crucially even, to the individual excellence of the members. The individual achievement of Ransom, of Tate, of Warren, of Davidson, of the others is related in a certain important way to their having lived in Nashville at a particular time, having been associated with Vanderbilt University, and having taken part in the regular meetings of the Fugitives.

Here, then, was something rare in American letters, something one tends to associate with European literature rather than our own—a collective outcropping of poetry, an organic society of poets, a community-wide literary endeavor, a Movement. One does not, for example, think to speak of the Harvard Poets; one speaks of Eliot, Cummings, Aiken, other individuals. Similarly, though one refers to the Chicago Poets, one is talking only of contributors to a magazine, for Sandburg, Masters, Lindsay did not customarily meet together, work in common, contribute directly to one another's technique. With the Nashville Fugitives, it was different—to an unusual degree they were a unit, a group; they shared a metaphysic and a poetic. Individuals though they were, with distinct styles and original attitudes, they seemed at the same time, in comparison with other poets of their epoch, to hold many more attitudes in common than one might have any right to expect among a group of American literary men.

THIS is not the appropriate occasion to attempt an assessment of the achievement of the Nashville Fugitives, or to essay comparisons of the excellences of the individual members. That much is being done by others, and may best be left to others. What is appropriate is an explanation of the circumstances that in May of 1956 drew a group of important American poets, together with some scholars, critics, and interested persons in general, to the campus of Vanderbilt University in Nashville for three days of recorded conversation, of which the present volume is a result. For on May 3-5, 1956, the Nashville Fugitives held a reunion, and while we who had persuaded them to reconvene sat listening, and while the microphones placed among them transmitted a steady flow of words to the recording tapes, the poets, the scholars, the businessmen and professional men who three decades earlier had published their little magazine in that same city talked away. They discussed what they had done, what they had failed to do, they reminisced over old times, they disputed, agreed.

They had come at the invitation of Vanderbilt University, and through the financial largesse of the Rockefeller Foundation, whose modest but sufficient grant to the American Studies Association had made the occasion possible. It was to be an attempt, a rather unprecedented, ambitious one at that, to record, and as it were "freeze in time," some American literary history. A group that had consorted together thirty and more years before, and the members of which had long since been dispersed and now lived and worked in places often thousands of miles apart, was to be reassembled in the surroundings where it had once functioned, and asked to reminisce about the old days and talk about poetry. The occasion would also provide Vanderbilt University, where most of the group had studied and some had taught, with the long-desired opportunity to pay homage to so distinguished a group of alumni. If all went well, it was reasoned, the result might furnish some information about the group that would otherwise be unobtainable, and might in addition provide a little insight into what made groups such as the Fugitives function.

It was in one sense an entirely artificial situation. For one does not turn back the clock merely by a temporary subverting of geography. These were not the same young men who had collaborated and clashed so momentously and fruitfully, back in the early 1920's. Far too many years had intervened, too many attitudes had become positions, too many individuals had since gone their own separate and positive ways, for the Fugitives ever to regain the full fervor and the cultural communality of their youth. To be precise, the poets who reassembled in Nashville in 1956 were middle-aged to elderly men, and their present identities included the accretion of active participation in more than three decades of literary, cultural, social, and political history, experienced not as a group but separately and in various ways.

There was even—and most of the Fugitives were quick to remark on it—a certain air of the mortuary about it all. "We are what the scholars call a *corpus*," Allen Tate remarked apprehensively at the first public session, "and we are about to be studied." Robert Penn Warren was even more skeptical: "A long time back at public executions, they let the culprit ride on his coffin while the band played a tune of his selection," he declared. ". . . it's like putting frog legs in the skillet in the grease in order to find how the frog felt when he jumped. The legs will twitch all right, but what are you learning?" The truth was that the individual Fugitives were both modest enough to feel quite uneasy at being made the subject of scholarly scrutiny, and proud enough to resent, just a little, the notion that what they had accomplished was quite ready yet for any sort of summing up. "After all," Allen Tate felt compelled to point out, "I am sure that we all hope to write something again."

Yet the fact was, and I believe that the text of the transcript shows it clearly, that to a certain extent at least, the Fugitive Conference of May 3-5, 1956, *was* successful in turning back the clock. For once the individual Fugitives were convened together behind closed doors, and the tape recorders began turning, something strange, even a little awesome, happened. They became a group again. The various individuals, despite some thirty years of separate and individual achievement, became the Nashville Fugitives once more. They began arguing, and the argument soon assumed, what was instantly and thrillingly recognizable to those who witnessed it, precisely the same lines of demarcation that had existed during the 1920's. Why, they began discussing, had none of the Fugitives succeeded in writing an epic? It was Tate, Ransom, Warren, Davidson, and Andrew Lytle on one side, Elliott and Alfred Starr on the other. The first five were those members of the Fugitives (though Lytle was not actually a Fugitive, he was subsequently so closely identified with the Vanderbilt group that for all intents and purpose he became one of them) who had gone on to become professional men of letters, who had committed themselves entirely and occupationally to literature. All of them assumed the position that for their time and place what had been required was an intense and fully committed use of language that demanded the highly self-conscious, concentrated discipline of the shorter poem. The epic, it was agreed, was possible only for an age in which a society agreed on a common myth, whereas their own society had possessed no such cohesion and unity. Their adversaries in debate, while in no sense denying the achievement of the individual Fugitives, took the position that things might have been otherwise, with the implied suggestion that by making their poetry "literary" and eschewing the bardic role, the Fugitives had arbitrarily restricted their influence and limited their scope.

What was at stake, as Cleanth Brooks intimated, was not simply whether one or more of the Fugitives might or might not have written an epic had he so desired, but more fundamental problems. The true point of contention, as one realizes more than ever after reading the transcript of the discussion, was whether the highly intellectual discipline that characterized the poetry of Ransom, Tate, Warren, and to a somewhat lesser extent, Davidson, was the proper strategy of poetry —in effect, whether "modern poetry" as typified in these men's work was defensible. It was the argument of the 1920's all over again, and the lines of cleavage were roughly the same as then.

Suffice it to say that the question was not settled. It was simply extended, clarified, developed. On the one side, William Yandell Elliott brought all his philosophical acumen and his far-ranging insight into social and cultural affairs eloquently into play. On the other, Allen Tate, Robert Penn Warren, Donald Davidson, John Crowe Ransom, maintained and advanced their zealous concern for the inviolability of language, their conviction of the intrinsic importance of the poem as poem. From a discussion of the epic, the topic shifted to other points. Sidney Mttron Hirsch made his appearance on the second day, and something of what the energizing effect of his subjective, mystical approach to poetry must have been for the other poets became apparent. The talk moved on to old times at Vanderbilt in the 1910's and 1920's, the teachers under whom the Fugitives had studied, the books they had read, the poets they had discussed and admired. On the final day the question of the Agrarian symposium *I'll Take My Stand*, to which some of the Fugitives had contributed, was raised for discussion, with all the problems of regional identity, clashing social, cultural, and political attitudes, the role of the man of letters in society, that were involved in that volume's history. When the final closed session ended, the Fugitives were battling away, the individual members holding their ground firmly and eloquently, in all the enjoyment of friendly dispute. The tape recorder, seemingly so inhibiting a factor when the sessions began, had long since been forgotten by the participants; they were too busy talking and having too good a time doing it. And whether or not the Fugitive conference of 1956 turns out to have produced any notable contribution to literary study, this much I think is undeniably true: the Fugitives themselves enjoyed it immensely.

WHAT did it all prove? One asks that question as he sits down to prepare an introduction to the published transcript, almost three years afterward. What is to be gleaned from the miles of recording tape, so faithfully and laboriously deciphered by Rob Roy Purdy and transcribed for this volume? Was the Rockefeller Foundation's experiment in supporting this attempt to "freeze history," as it were, for the benefit of future scholarship, a worthwhile endeavor?

We do not know, of course, what the future importance of the Nashville Fugitives, whether as a group or as individual poets, novelists, and critics, will be in American literary and intellectual history. If, let us say, a three-day meeting had been staged in the city of Dublin in Ireland in the year 1930, and such writers as Yeats, Russell, Hyde, Dunsany, and Lady Gregory had been willing to discuss their times and their work, there now seems little doubt but that literary scholarship would have been much enriched. Can we claim as much for the Nashville Fugitives?

The Fugitives themselves would be (and indeed, have been) the first to scout such an evaluation of their merits. Yet, without attempting any comparisons of relative importance, it does seem difficult to imagine that, a half-century from now, there will not be considerable historical interest in the Southern literary renascence of the 1920's and thereafter—or that the transcript of a meeting at which Warren, Tate, Ransom, Davidson, Elliott, and the others sat around for several days and discussed their times and their work will not contain much of interest to the future student of American literary and cultural history. At any rate, to the Rockefeller Foundation, to the American Studies Association, to Vanderbilt University, even, despite due modesty, to the individual Fugitives themselves, it seemed worth the effort.

Looking at the occasion now, as one privileged to sit in on the meetings and now charged with composing this introduction to the published transcript, the present writer would venture to set forth some few observations as to what the uses of the occasion may have been. In so doing, as indeed throughout these introductory remarks, he speaks for himself alone.

First, specific historical information was brought out, and critical insights into the problems under discussion were developed during the sessions themselves. Certain valuable facts were recalled about the actual circumstances and events surrounding the organization of the Fugitives, and the publication of *The Fugitive,* during the early 1920's. These are set forth in the transcript, and will henceforth be available as a matter of record.

Second, some insight was provided into the individual participants themselves, as they developed their own ideas and responded to other ideas during the meetings. Studying the transcript, we can see a group of highly articulate men thinking aloud, so to speak, on a number of interesting points at issue, and thus we can understand the modes of thought of these poets a little better. Indeed, the conversational style and tone of the text, retaining as it does the actual flavor of discussion without the rounded perorations of more formal utterance, enhance this possibility.

Third, a striking picture was afforded of the Fugitives as a group. They did not hesitate to assail one another's ideas; they were courteous, polite, but they did not stand on ceremony. They were not awed by distinctions of reputation or age (save possibly, I think, in the response of some of the poets to Sidney Hirsch). There was little or no complacency among them, no tendency toward smugness. The argument about the epic was a revealing demonstration of the humility of the group as a whole. All were quite ready to examine the question of whether, by not producing an epic, they had failed in their role as poets. It did not seem to occur to any of them that their entire life's work, both as individuals and as a group, should not properly be laid open to complete assessment by their fellows. Indeed, from time to time it was necessary for those present who were not Fugitives to remind them of what seemed obvious to us—that there was a certain inappropriateness for a group of poets who had achieved so much to spend their time discussing why they had failed to produce epic poems, instead of examining the nature of their achievement in the verse forms they *had* chosen to work in. Some of us were even a little impatient at the spectacle of Allen Tate, John Crowe Ransom, Robert Penn Warren, Donald Davidson, and the others using the better part of a full evening's session examining what they seemed to consider their possible failure to produce something that not a single member of the group had ever set out to accomplish!

Fourth, the dynamics, so to speak, of the Fugitive group were revealed in action. For those of us who watched, it was exciting to see how each of the Fugitives drew profit from the insights of the others, how a structure of ideas was pyramided, so to speak, as each member's responses helped another to develop his own ideas still further. One caught a glimpse, for all the three decades of separate achievement that had intervened, of how dynamic a group they were, of what being a Fugitive meant for each one of them, of what it meant to be one of a group of gifted, enthusiastic young writers possessed of a cultural and historical background roughly homogenous in nature. One got a sense of what it must have been like to have one's ideas tested and tempered by the insights of one's peers—what it must have been like, in short, to have been a young man writing poetry at Vanderbilt University in Nashville, Tennessee, during the years 1920-1925.

Hollins College, Virginia,
January, 1959.

FIRST SESSION

Thursday Evening, May 3

Moderator: CLEANTH BROOKS

BROOKS: I think we are ready to start. I must remind you of several things, something that I wish I didn't have to remind you of: that our voices are being recorded on tape. We'd better try to talk one at a time. It strikes me that this is a kind of parable—we have all been making parables today—of the situation of the poet in the modern world. It has its good points and its bad. We have an audience—perhaps posterity, who knows? On the other hand it is a kind of intimate talk in public. And that may very well be a constricting force; and, I submit, may be a kind of parable of the poet's plight today. You are surely sensible of the absurdity of my position. I can assure you that I am sensible of it. A group of this sort doesn't need a moderator. Something which is a natural spring, arising as it arises, flowing its own sweet will—it's not an artesian well, Pegasus can't be a circus horse put through tricks. A living community—something that was a community and one is inclined to think is still a living community—can't be treated as some kind of mechanical structure. I am perfectly aware of all that and expect to have you prove to my satisfaction very quickly that the community exists, that it doesn't need any moderators. People talk, and the ball will be passed from person to person. This much I shall ask you to remember, or I may do myself: that is to try to identify people. If you can remember, if you are picking up a point or giving a rejoinder, to mention the person's name, it will help a good deal if somebody ever does get down to the tape and transcribes it.

STARR: Has the moderator identified himself?

BROOKS: No, but this is Cleanth Brooks, starting this session. To repeat what I said a moment ago, this is the absurdity of the position: what I should like to do is to make you forget all about the tape or any microphones in the room. Let's do the best we can, hoping that the sheer dynamic of the group will overcome the business of having to have moderators, even the presence of the microphones. Already, it seems to me—and I am completely delighted at this—that the two or three things which I am told the Rockefeller Foundation wanted to have us talk about have already been got at quickly and promptly, spontaneously, in the papers already given. Presumably they will come up. I was particularly interested, as all of us were, in some of Donald Davidson's remarks this evening on the problems of the poet, the problems of our civilization. I think, myself, that many of the problems which he mentioned, his problems for the poet, turn out to be problems of civilization. Would you agree to something of that sort, Don? Would you push your point through further?

DAVIDSON: Yes, what I said was what I've been gradually teaching myself by attempting to teach my classes.

TATE: Well, Mr. Moderator, Don is continuing a debate this evening we've had for more than thirty years [*laughter*] and—

DAVIDSON: No question about that, Allen.

TATE: Yes. So I think that my answer would be now what it was thirty years ago: that we haven't got a choice between literary poetry, as you describe it, and this pure Pierian spring, folk literature. It's a choice between literary poetry or none at all: the canned poetry, manufactured for a super-bourgeois society. And I disagree on another point: I don't think that poetry, by any means, has exhausted its techniques. I think probably this school of modern poetry, that we call the "poetic revolution of the twentieth century," has come more or less to an end. But no doubt there will be other poets to surprise us later.

BROOKS: Would you say, Allen, that we are probably already spreading out into a kind of period style?

TATE: Very much so, yes.

BROOKS: I am frequently reminded of what you've got in the very happy period—it seems to me—the seventeenth century, when even the third and fourth rate poets pick up a tone, set it, maintain it, and so on. And I think that, even if that seems a little dull because standard and common, it may be a very high achievement. And we had better be glad that we—

TATE: Sometimes you're inclined to pick up the literary magazines; you read a poem, and say "this is pretty good," and then you turn the page and—

BROOKS: Quite. Quite right.

TATE: —it sort of runs into the next poem. They all run together. But it's all highly accomplished.

DAVIDSON: Well, Allen, in the complete paper, from which I read only the conclusion, I pointed out that I developed the defense of poetry that you and John and Cleanth and others have been giving, and pointed out that it started as a necessity in the late sixteenth century—

TATE: That's right.

DAVIDSON: —at the same time that the literary poetry begins; and that it included not only the defense of poetry itself, but necessarily the attack of the poets on the society which had gotten itself into difficulties, not merely because it was hostile to the poets, but because it was disintegrating, itself. It was necessary for the poets, therefore, to make an attack on society. And, of course, we have done that, you see. Every defense of poetry that has been made, no matter what the form—whether in one of John's most aesthetic essays, or in some of the Agrarian essays in a more direct form—there is always the intuitive approach to the evils of the society. So that has to be taken into account, and I do take it into account in the consideration I have tried to give to the subject.

BETHURUM: But when was there not, Don? When was poetry sufficiently in tune with the society?

DAVIDSON: Any time before the sixteenth century. As far back as you can go.

BETHURUM: Not the fourteenth.

DAVIDSON: Well, there were temporary lapses. But the fourteenth and fifteenth centuries were certainly a period of the flowering of a certain kind of tradition of poetry. You're thinking of the big figures. There were no big figures.

BETHURUM: Well, I'm thinking of Langland, Chaucer. Both in that society were pretty big, I would think.

BROOKS: If I may put in to identify the speaker, Dorothy Bethurum was giving a kind of moral: What was she, an old medievalist, doing at this meeting? And I reproached her, telling her that maybe a medievalist was exactly what we needed when we considered the points—

DAVIDSON: Well, my objection to the medieval scholar's position is that the medieval scholar is too often studying the poetry of that time in the light of poetry of later centuries, and trying to find it literary when it is not.

TATE: Well, what do you mean by literary, now?

DAVIDSON: I mean adapted to the book, as I indicated. A manuscript book is very different from a printed book. The change sets in when printing begins.

BETHURUM: I don't see that there's any difference between Chaucer's being literary—which I think he was—and the seventeenth century poets' being literary. Of course they didn't do the same sort of thing, but Chaucer was as conscious a traditionalist as you can find.

DAVIDSON: Well, the society in which Chaucer wrote was dominated by a tradition that was rather oral than non-oral, and in which poetry linked with all the other arts.

BETHURUM: Well, yes—

DAVIDSON: You define him as literary, and I wouldn't deny that he is; a Chaucerian kind of poetry could not possibly be written in the sixteenth century or the seventeenth century. That is, you can't return to that style, unless you are willing to have a society that will provide the base for a Chaucerian type of poetry.

BETHURUM: Well, I think Eliot is a literary man in the way that Chaucer wasn't; in that, I would say, experience is not as vital to him as it was to Chaucer. But if you mean dependence on books, hardly anybody could be more dependent than Chaucer.

DAVIDSON: Well, I'll take one point: Chaucer didn't have to bother about being original. He wrote in the style that was prevalent all the way through, from the ballad. He took freely from other poets without giving them credit. In other words, poetry that circulated was common coin, and the mark of the author didn't have to be on it. With the modern author of the book, that is not true: the mark of the author has to be on it. It's copyrighted.

BETHURUM: At least he was pretty careful to give credit— oh, he sometimes gave the wrong credit—but he was awfully careful to acknowledge his books. More so than most of his contemporaries, I admit.

TATE: Well, Don, it seems to me that the argument for a unity of the arts in which no one artist becomes so highly developed and specialized leaves out both the better music and the better words. Wyatt was a very fine lyric poet and his poems could be sung. But suppose that music were arrested at that point: we should never have had the great nineteenth-century music we know, like Beethoven, or some modern music. This loss of unity is almost necessary for the development of the particular art. We couldn't sing John Donne's "A Valediction, Forbidding Mourning."

DAVIDSON: But there are others of John Donne that you can sing and that were sung.

TATE: Yes, that's quite true—

DAVIDSON: They were set to music by Ferrabosco—

TATE: Yes, and Donne was at that turning point.

DAVIDSON: Yes.

TATE: And at the same time we couldn't sing a Beethoven quartet. Or would you rather have it so?

DAVIDSON: No, I merely point out the phenomenon. Music develops in its own sphere—a separate sphere—from the seventeenth century on.

TATE: Yes.

THORP: Well, Don, haven't you got something else very interesting happening, though, right here? Many of our students buy recordings of the poets reading their poetry. I go into the music shop on the square, and there along with the latest recordings of classical music, or music dealing with jazz, will be Dylan Thomas, the Library of Congress Poets, Robert Frost. Frost comes to town, and packs Alexander Hall. Almost any poet that is known at all—who comes to the campus—can get out a big audience; I think that this is something phenomenal in our time and just beginning.

TATE: Thirteen thousand, seven hundred people came to hear T. S. Eliot in Minneapolis when he was there this spring.

BROOKS: I am very glad that Willard Thorp has just put in what he has about the interest in oral arts, because it's the sort of thing, it's the sort of evidence, that inclines me to take Don's comment on oral art as symptomatic and metaphorical rather than literal. It seems to me that you don't really get at the basis of things that way. I have a friend who says that the age of the printed book is over. He says he's already given it a name—the Gutenberg period is finished. [*laughter*] Television is taking over. On the other hand, if he is right, and there is perhaps a little core of truth in what he is saying—I am talking, Allen, about Marshall McLuhan—

TATE: Yes.

BROOKS: —and if the age of Gutenberg is over, if the age of the printed book is past, then still this age of television is not going to suit Don, and it's not going to suit me. And it's not going to suit this problem.

DAVIDSON: No, it doesn't suit because it's a substitute for the real thing.

BROOKS: Yes.

DAVIDSON: And this means something like what Cleanth says, no doubt. But a good deal of this interest might be described as biographical, you see; they want the album by Robert Frost or somebody because they have studied him, and they want some sense of the man, the history. That's as near as they can come to getting the presence. I once told Robert Frost—and he didn't like it at all—that a good part of the effect of his poetry depended on the fact that he was partly in the oral tradition. And he just didn't like it. He wanted to be thought of as Horace, I suppose. Something of the sort. [*laughter*]

ELLIOTT: Don, I think that's entirely natural. Everybody likes to be something that he isn't, in some sense; and Robert Frost is rather conscious of his own limitations, too. The question I'd like to put to this group, which is after all the group of Fugitives, is what were the dividing lines in our own *ars poetica*, critical poetic, in the beginning? And it seems to me that you sketched out some of them quite adequately. The bardic tradition, if you can call it that—and I used to try to send over people that I thought would be good for you from Oxford, like Yeats and some of the real bards, the people who were in the tradition we are talking about and who were still very literary poets, too, I mean. I think there is no essential contradiction between the two things, and it seems to me this comment about television may have a real importance. I just finished a book on it, curiously enough. If you are going to cry out against the times—which is the fashion for poets and always is—what the poet should do is to do something more than cry out against the times. Now that is what the Fugitives set themselves to do, I think. They had some ideas that the roots of poetry lay in metaphysics very deeply. An absent member of the group had a very important part to play in it: Sidney Hirsch isn't here, but my memory is that Sidney's discourses on Plato and the mystery of religions had a very important part in the formation of the Fugitives, long before we began publishing anything. As Don said, when we were still meeting at the Calumet Club,* and just casually out at people's houses and things of that sort. And this metaphysical tradition about poetry was at least a contribution that had a common pull on us. But we split rather early on whether or not poetry was to be bardic as well as literary. And Don— and I think I was associated myself with his line of thinking on that—kept to the idea that poetry should have a—very much of a—musical content, and that we were compressing into the acrobatics of poetry the things that everybody wanted to learn in those days. The Fugitives were particularly active under John Ransom's leadership and Allen Tate's. And a new kind of acrobatics—if I can put it that

* An undergraduate literary club at Vanderbilt.

way—an entire repudiation of the sentimentality of the tradition. But what was the most important thing from my point of view was that we lost the epic in poetry. And none of us ever had very much courage about pursuing that. Some of us did try to write them, but nobody would ever bother to listen to a poem that was as long as an epic had to be. And this was one of the rocks on which we really split pretty thoroughly. And then we got off into criticism because we couldn't say in poetry the things that poetry might well have said. Andrew Lytle wrote *Bedford Forrest and His Critter Company,* and then it became the fashion to write at least the life of one Confederate general by the more active members of the group. [*laughter*] The "Ode to the Confederate Dead," done in rather tight form by Allen, was symptomatic of something that was happening. But the epic poem, which I should have hoped might have come out of this group, was something we worked up to very rarely. I think Don got awfully close to it in "Lee in the Mountains," which is to my mind one of the great poems that came out of this group. There were beginnings of them, but why is it that a natural development of metaphysical poetry connected with the epic—which Johnny studied in Milton and gave us many interesting insights into—didn't come out of this group? I put that as an interesting question that has always puzzled me.

RANSOM: But I would think the answer to that would be that no one knows how to write an epic and no modern has done it, and Red Warren writes a very powerful poem—long poem—but I would dare say it's not an epic, it's—

ELLIOTT: That's right.

RANSOM: —it's not the heroic. And it simply isn't a heroic age. I would think it's as simple as that: that a poet just can't bring himself to try an epic, that he doesn't command that kind of perspective—

ELLIOTT: What's the reason, Johnny?

RANSOM: We're not simplified to that degree.

ELLIOTT: Why? This is the question that I—

RANSOM: Because it's a very intricate society, with a great many little pockets, rather than a single uniformity of culture, and because they are problematic at almost every stage. And the intellect has gotten into everything, and the epic poet assumes, I think, an age of common consent to a great consensus of opinion on the topics.

ELLIOTT: Well, Johnny, I don't believe that's true to your own analysis of Milton. Milton was far from being an anti-intellectual poet; and he was certainly a man who was complex in his thinking, wasn't he?

RANSOM: Yes, but that's by courtesy an epic; that's after the age of epics.

TATE: Is it a real epic?

RANSOM: It's not a real epic. [*general murmur*]

ELLIOTT: Well, what is an epic? I think that's a very interesting question to hand out in this kind of group, because by common consent it's something we didn't do and apparently couldn't do. What is an epic? It's the trial of a hero, isn't it?

RANSOM: Well, I used to read Ker and others on the epic, and as I understand it, the epic arises as the expression of a nation which has gone through its strife. And it's the representation of the struggle to maintain its ideals and to express its religion and its culture and its heroism.

ELLIOTT: That's right.

RANSOM: And—

ELLIOTT: This is the answer to the times—

RANSOM: I beg your pardon?

ELLIOTT: This is the answer to the times. An epic is an attempt to create an answer to the times. Instead of just crying out on them, an epic tries to shape them. And if we are not going to fight lost causes all our lives, the poets have to meet this challenge in some sense in modern society.

RANSOM: I can think of long poems being done, and especially dramas, but it's pretty hard to think of an epic in classical terms being done.

ELLIOTT: Well, you've had a half dozen really memorable efforts of turning Lincoln into something of a good poem. The fact is, however, that nobody has ever done an epic on him. And is this a measure of the times? Our brother Andrew Lytle has done a number of works that could have been epics just as well as novels about the Spanish in this country.

LYTLE: In that form, though, Bill—

ELLIOTT: Well, I'm just asking you.

RANSOM: Well, I would think Mr. Warren ought to speak to that question. Now I know that—

ELLIOTT: I wish he would.

RANSOM: —before he published the long poem, *Brother to Dragons*, he spoke of why he found that that was not to be represented best in the form of prose fiction, that it would take the poem. I don't think he quite conceived it as an epic, but I would like very much to hear what went through his mind, what he thought of.

WARREN: It never crossed my mind I was trying to write an epic, I'll say that. [*laughter and murmurs*]

ELLIOTT: And he didn't write one.

WARREN: Well, if I had, it would have been by inadvertence.

TATE: Now, we have some very learned scholars here. I would like some information. We'd have first to count up the number of epics that have survived in print, and the number of epics which are really first rate. I should think there are about three in Western literature. And even the third one, Vergil's *Aeneid*, is pretty delayed, late, yes.

BETHURUM: Well, you can't have, can you Bill, an epic about a hero in any period of a civilization except a very early one? And when you get a—

TATE: Almost a tribal civilization.

BETHURUM: Yes. When you get a late poem, when you get a literary epic, like the *Aeneid* or like *Paradise Lost,* it isn't about a hero, it's about a cause. And—

ELLIOTT: Well, it's still an epic.

BETHURUM: Well, yes, but might it have a cause, now? Only it's very hard to find a standard-bearer big enough.

ELLIOTT: Well, this is the failure of the poets, as metaphysical poets, who are discerning the values of a civilization in a creative and a therapeutic way, if I may say so—

BETHURUM: Yes.

ELLIOTT: —if they are going to be the physicians of a society. If they are just going to be the diagnosticians and follow T. S. Eliot through the Waste Land, and the rest of the things that he—

RANSOM: You can get a testament of beauty as Bridges did, but that is in no sense an epic, but a rather comprehensive, philosophical evaluation of what man has come to, I suppose. And that seems practical.

THORP: I don't suppose Robinson's long poems are in any sense to be called epic or heroic, are they? They're dramatic verse, if anything.

ELLIOTT: Actually, there have been a number of efforts at epics. They've not been too successful. Archie MacLeish tried in *Conquistador* to do something of a sustained poem

that had some elements of this, but he didn't have it in
him—

TATE: But there was no action in that poem whatever. The
old hero wound up sorry for himself.

ELLIOTT: Exactly.

TATE: That's all he was doing throughout the poem.

ELLIOTT: And this is the point I am really trying to make:
the poets are really diagnosticians and not creators. And
is it possible that our times are so completely out of joint
that that's the case?

WARREN: Bill, I don't accept your distinction.

ELLIOTT: Well, let's see why not.

WARREN: I think you're just making it awfully easy for yourself, the way I look at it.

ELLIOTT: Well, I'm making it hard for you. [*laughter*] It
would have been by inadvertence, I believe, your handling—

WARREN: I feel no compulsion. It just doesn't interest me.
[*murmurs*] Definitely, I don't feel any compulsion to try
to write a poem. [*amidst general murmur*] And you don't
worry about whether you're going to call it an epic or "X."

ELLIOTT: What we started out—

WARREN: You try to say something in the best way you can.

ELLIOTT: Let me put it this way—

WARREN: Your concern isn't there, I think, with trying to
write. And what I was quarreling about was the distinction
between diagnostics and creation, because *The Waste Land*
as a diagnostic poem is as much a creation to me as, well
say, a poem like—what? *Lycidas?* Is that one of the better
creative poems?

ELLIOTT: That's right; it's a creative poem.

TATE: You don't think *The Waste Land* is—

ELLIOTT: I don't think *Samson Agonistes* is a creative poem.

WARREN: I don't see the distinction, you see. I think they are both at the same level, not in value, necessarily. Though I would be willing to argue that on another occasion, perhaps. But they belong to the same kind of—*Lycidas* is as much a diagnostic poem, a critical poem, as it is a creative poem.

ELLIOTT: Well, I'm just trying to untangle something—

WARREN: And it's a real wrangle with the world at large. And more of a wrangle—more explicitly a wrangle than any of this is.

ELLIOTT: Well, this is probably true. But it had in it the elements of some suggestions about where the wrangle wanted to come out of the society. This is the thing that, I think, we've confessed by default, in a way: that we don't think it's the poet's function to set the world to rights any more, or to set up a standard, so to speak, in symbolism.

TATE: How do we know Homer set out to do that, Bill?

ELLIOTT: I don't think we know it, but we know that he accented certain virtues; that those were the virtues that his society regarded as virtues to be imitated. This is the essence of an epic.

TATE: I think we've got a point here, then. What are the virtues valued by modern Western society? They aren't virtues that a critical intelligence is going to acknowledge, to any great extent. And therefore you get the poets a little disgruntled about it all.

BROOKS: Would you give an illustration, Allen? I think it would be useful.

TATE: Well, I think *The Waste Land* would be a very good

example. John's poetry is a very good example. Practically all of us who have written poetry find ourselves—I think without any degree of self-consciousness—in that situation. We don't have to think it out and arrive at that position. That's just where we find ourselves.

RANSOM: Well, there's one other thing, it seems to me, in our minds—certainly in mine. I shouldn't know how to do a long poem. And really what I would rather see, rather find, or rather get if possible, would be a lyric effect. We tend to laugh a little at Poe's destructive analysis of the long poem, but in better words we would all make the same point, I think.

TATE: Very much, yes.

ELLIOTT: That has been the prevailing tone of the Fugitives; there isn't any question about it. This is the essence of what the contribution of the Fugitives did: they were, essentially, people who showed up what they regarded as a false tradition. I think that's perfectly justifiable, and perfectly right. But it is of great interest to me that there should not be values in Western society that we regard as capable of being symbolized. I think Don did try to symbolize some of them. We may not have agreed with him—

TATE: I certainly acknowledge my admiration for "The Tall Men," but it would not, through any stretch of the meaning of the word, "act." This fine poem is highly subjective, complicated, introspective. And the actions are allusive: there are allusions to action—to heroic actions in the past.

ELLIOTT: How about "Lee in the Mountains"?

TATE: It's the same thing.

ELLIOTT: No, I don't think it is. I think that there you've got something—

DAVIDSON: If I could put in a word, I would have to agree with Allen there, because "The Tall Men" is more subjective than narrative. It just has bits of narrative in it, in the first place. And "Lee in the Mountains" is not narrative: it's a meditative poem. It seems to me that we are right back where we were about thirty-five years ago. We've just picked up where we left off. [*laughter*] But—

ELLIOTT: That's what I intended. [*laughter and general murmur*]

DAVIDSON: Well, I would like to make one point about Milton. I just want to get it in somehow. It may not be a true epic, but the low-grade effect of Milton's poem, as an epic, is not to be underestimated. And what I am saying is that the eighteenth-century poets abstracted from Milton a so-called "Miltonic style" which they used to some extent. But the death of the epic as far as they were concerned is illustrated in Pope's "Rape of the Lock," which is in effect an essay on the topic that you can't write an epic any more because the society won't have it. But, meanwhile, Milton's scheme of mythology, his conceptions, supplied to Protestantism the visual images that Puritanism threw overboard when it abjured Papistry. So that in the conceptions of people who had never read Milton's poem, you see, the idea of angels, the idea of Adam and Eve, and of Satan in particular, took on a Miltonic form. And I would, therefore, say that his poem had the influence in our culture that an epic would have, and it was the last poem of that character in our language to achieve such an effect, and that none of the quasi-epical poems that have followed, or the narrative poems, have had such an effect on our culture at large, you see. I think that point ought to be made. And then as to Homer, you have to remember that it's a question whether Homer wrote his poem or whether writing was used at all. It was composed for performance and was carried in memory, impossible as it may seem to us, and was recited at festival occasions. And we no longer have festival occasions comparable to that. Now the fact that some of our early literary poetry in the sixteenth century begins to take on a colloquial style, shows a recognition that they still wanted it to have an oral effect. You see, the colloquial effect in John Donne—and then Merrill has it in his sonnets—relies strongly on that. They are book poems in a sense, but they do employ that colloquial idiom; and, therefore, sort of pass over into a kind of oral form. And wherever the poets are trying that now—various poets are—it seems to me that's a grasping after a condition of spoken performance which we don't get very much of, actually. I'd just like to put in those footnotes to the discussion, that's all.

BROOKS: Well, they're very interesting footnotes indeed, Don. I would like to add one point, something I'm sure you've thought of. I think that the case of William Butler Yeats here is instructive. I never can read Yeats' autobiography without finding myself doing a running commentary on the South. I mean everything that he ran into, one can find an analogy for right around here. There was a man who tried very hard to write an epic, who believed in the oral values, who somehow won through at the end to a new kind of, oh, lyric quality. But the fact that he fought such a drawn battle, or worse, with the epic and finally gave it up in favor of a certain kind of lyric, may be another indication of the difficulty modern poets are up against.

DAVIDSON: Well, Cleanth, I said in what I read to the group at the dinner—and very carefully put it in—that the poetry that we could come to would combine some oral and some literary qualities.

BROOKS: Yes.

DAVIDSON: And that is actually happening. That is, *The Waste Land* wouldn't be as good as it is, if it didn't have some oral qualities in it.

BROOKS: I quite agree. I quite agree.

DAVIDSON: And John's best poems, his most memorable

lyric poems, have a certain dramatic speaking quality that some of his other more literary poems don't have, and it's those that have the dramatic quality that are the most valid and the most memorable. And the same would be true of Allen's, and also of Red's, and any others. I think right now that—if you could take some sort of straw vote on it, if there were any way of doing it—you would find that those are the poems that tend to cling to the memory whereas the others have to be studied and worked up.

BROOKS: I—Excuse me. Go ahead, John, please.

RANSOM: Well, it seems to me that we ought to give some recognition to the fact that we have a new art, which would take some of the responsibility off poetry, and that's fiction.

TATE: Yes.

RANSOM: It's inconceivable that we could have a poetic version of *Moby Dick*.

TATE: Or of *The Wings of the Dove*.

RANSOM: Or *The Wings of the Dove*. [*laughter*]

DAVIDSON: And that is entirely dependent on the book. Without the book it couldn't exist at all.

TATE: Well, I don't know. [*general murmuring among Davidson, Bethurum, Tate*]

ELLIOTT: How about *Billy Budd*? *Billy Budd* is disguised poetry, with very thinly disguised character.

RANSOM: Well, in a long narrative—

ELLIOTT: And the play that has been done from this, you see. I mean this is—

BROOKS: Let me break in to say that Bill Elliott has been coming through with a great deal of very interesting stuff, and nobody is identifying him, please. Please mention Bill so that we can get him on the tape. Go ahead, I've interrupted.

RANSOM: Can't that be stuck in?

BROOKS: [*amidst general murmur*] Well, we'll probably dub it in. [*laughter*]

ELLIOTT: I refuse to be dubbed. [*laughter*]

STEVENSON: Could I butt in at this moment, Cleanth, to return to a somewhat more elemental question it seemed to me we slid over rather rapidly just as I came in here? And that question was whether it was really difficult or not to produce epic poetry due to the lack of simplicity of the age. I got the impression that that was not regarded very highly as an argument. But it seems to me that if we could sit here this evening and say, or even consider, that the age of Gutenberg had come to a close, we could also say that so has the age of Vasco da Gama.

BROOKS: I don't think the age of Gutenberg has come to a close. I was—

STEVENSON: No.

BROOKS: —just quoting my friend.

STEVENSON: But as a matter for argument, I'd go on and say this: if heroism, in either the individual or the national sense, is an essential element of heroic and epic poetry, then it quite obviously has become much more difficult to be a hero either individually or nationally than it was in an age when the issues were simpler and more easily decided. So that perhaps the poets themselves are not falling down in their function. Or their function has to be, as has been said here more recently, interpreted in different terms.

TATE: Well, Cleanth, couldn't we cite a single, very ambitious work of our century, an attempt to write, if not an epic, a great panorama of the War Between the States— the late Steve Benêt's *John Brown's Body*? Now the trouble with that poem seems to me to be that, in the first place, the language is vulgar and coarse—Benêt had no ear—and he was able to present a big panorama at the expense of other things that poetry ought to have. Homer is not coarse. I should think only a very naïve person could take *John Brown's Body* without suffering a little bit on every page.

BROOKS: I quite agree.

DAVIDSON: I'd like to qualify that.

BROOKS: How would you qualify it, Don?

DAVIDSON: Not a completely naïve person. A completely naïve person would reject it utterly. It's the pseudo-literary person.

BROOKS: Yes, I agree.

ELLIOTT: Yes, but is it substantially impossible to write something on the War Between the States in a poetic—an acceptably poetic—vein, that would not have the putty in it that everybody recognizes in *John Brown's Body*?

TATE: I think you're quite right. I think it *is* possible.

ELLIOTT: Well, then, the query that I return to—and I'm not going to do more than just suggest it and leave it, because I wrote a poem once called "Critica Poetica" which I read to Johnny once, upholding the exact thesis that you are now attacking, that as poets you are like witch doctors— you are out of date: take off your headdresses, medicine men, and so on, and revert to honest prose. If you can write a myth as rich as Plato's *Ur* and so on, why not do it? What is there to prevent it? This is the thing that really interests me; and I think it's a fundamental lack of any understanding on the part of the poets at being able to discern values in their society that they think are worth perpetuating. You see, if this is the case, it indicates a certain bankruptcy of that element, and the Fugitives set themselves in a very limited fashion in their Agrarian period and in their neo-Confederate period to reaffirm certain values. Now it's very interesting they didn't do it in poetry. That's the question, Don.

RUBIN: It seems to me that they did.

ELLIOTT: Well, now, which ones? Let's name some.

BROOKS: What do you say about that, Mr. Rubin? Give us some illustrations.

RUBIN: Well—

BROOKS: Just getting you on the tape.

RUBIN: I think the "Ode to the Confederate Dead" is an example.

BROOKS: Exactly.

ELLIOTT: Well—

RUBIN: And I could name ten more.

ELLIOTT: And you could name pieces, occasional pieces.

RUBIN: Well, I think Mr. Warren's long poem is a pretty large occasional piece.

ELLIOTT: Yes, I agree. It's a large occasional piece. But is it the affirmation of any—I think it's still a diagnostic piece, a piece of handling, if I correctly interpret it, and I have a right to an opinion on it. If you are talking about *Brother to Dragons,* this is a very important piece of poetry, but it doesn't take the form that they found necessary in *I'll Take My Stand* and other affirmations of that sort to say what they thought was good for the society, what was the way to follow. I didn't happen to share that, when I'm the only Fugitive that supports a farm, to my knowledge, to this day. [*laughter*]

DAVIDSON: The reason why they couldn't do that in a narrative or dramatic or epic poem was that in those things you have to be able to say what everybody already knows and accepts. In a society that's divided against itself, the poet is in a difficult position. [*general murmur*]

ELLIOTT: Well, this is the closest thing to an answer we've had yet.

DAVIDSON: And that's the whole trouble in the matter. That's why you can't write an epic. That's part of it, and the other part is that you can't use the form of the epic because the form of the epic is intended for performance, not for a book, you see, except as the book is there to record it and to assist the memory. If it can't be performed aloud, it's not an epic; and Milton—you remember again—Milton started his poem as a drama.

ELLIOTT: Nobody has yet talked about Dante. And I would suppose that any immediate outcries about—

DAVIDSON: The specialist on Dante is sitting right by me. That's Allen Tate.

ELLIOTT: Well, of course, and I'm just trying to bait Allen into saying something else.

TATE: Well, Bill, you wouldn't describe the *Divine Comedy* as an epic, would you?

ELLIOTT: I think that it has many of the qualities of an epic in that it holds up values which are to be imitated, and it goes through the entire categorization of the struggle of various heroes. It hasn't got a single hero, however.

TATE: It seems to me it's almost as sophisticated in its method as Henry James' *The Ambassadors*.

ELLIOTT: Yes.

TATE: There's a central intelligence; everything happens in Dante's mind. He sees countless people, but they are not— they are glanced at and heard for a few moments and passed over for somebody else. I like Francis Fergusson's phrase, the sub-title to his book on the *Purgatorio*, "Dante's Drama of the Mind." He's very modern indeed.

ELLIOTT: There's no question about that.

TATE: And the trouble about all these people, except a few people in the *Paradiso,* is that although they had engaged in these heroic actions, there was always something wrong with it. Dante was cutting under them all the time. And, for example, the whole conception of sin complicated his characters and subject—something that Homer didn't seem to go into so much.

ELLIOTT: That's quite right. It was a different type of epic, and there were values that were implicit in Dante. I think you wouldn't deny that. Well, I know Dante's in our time. This is the other—

TATE: No, modern poets go to Dante for odds and ends.

ELLIOTT: Yes, that's right. Odds and ends is just about right —snappers-up of unconsidered trifles. The grand scale—the architectonic design, the reduction of something to a thing that's comparable. Don kept talking about Wagner, and in whatever low esteem you may hold Wagner as an artist— and it's fashionable to do so—he did have a grand design.

TATE: Well, now Don made a point a minute ago which would apply to the *Divine Comedy.* The scheme of redemption was accepted by practically everybody in Dante's time. But all Dante had to do was project it in the framework of the Ptolemaic cosmos. And everybody knew where every character was located, not only visually but in the scheme of salvation.

ELLIOTT: Well, Allen, you are so much greater an authority on Dante than anybody around here—

TATE: Why, I'm no authority on Dante. I can scarcely read him.

ELLIOTT: —that I venture with extreme caution the suggestion that Dante was not altogether in the complete acceptance of all the values of his time, but from time to time he was introducing the most modern doubts in the business involving Paolo and Francesca; you can't quite feel that he was happy about them floating in the abyss—

TATE: Oh, no, he didn't like it at all—

ELLIOTT: That's right, and there were suggestions there of a different kind of value in spite of these—

DAVIDSON: What would you say, Allen, to the fact that Dante wrote in Italian rather than in Latin?

TATE: I think that is a very important thing. Latin had ceased to be the language of immediate experience.

DAVIDSON: It was the language of literature.

TATE: Yes, but it is the language of a literature that was no longer closely related to the common experience of the people of Italy. Latin was no longer the language of the affections. It was an official language, a literary language. And Dante saw that; in fact, he makes that very point, in one of the epistles.

BROOKS: What are the virtues—let me put the matter in— that the whole society really believes in?

ELLIOTT: That's the real question.

BROOKS: I think you will find them in Ernest Hemingway, and I think that he's probably about as close to an epic as we have. [*murmurs of "no," etc.*] I think it's a mighty poor —[*murmurs*] No, no, I mean it's actually what I say: I think it's a mighty poor little epic. But we believe in a certain kind of honesty, at least we all admire it. We believe in a certain kind of courage—

TATE: I admire it as far as it goes.

BROOKS: My admiration is very moderate, but what I am saying is— [*general murmur and conversation*]

ELLIOTT: I think there was a period in which going to Hell roaring was at least being better than pathetic and damned in the Fitzgerald style.

BROOKS: Sure.

STARR: Particularly with hair on your chest.

ELLIOTT: That's right, and this is some kind of a virtue, let's admit that. But it's not quite the *summum bonum* of Western society.

BROOKS: I quite agree, but that's my tiny little contribution to the problem, that if one wants this sort of thing, about all the basis we've got is what Hemingway is doing. The New York stage has two formulas that are necessary for a success—

ELLIOTT: Well now by—

BROOKS: —civil rights and sexual emancipation; those aren't the things we all believe in.

ELLIOTT: This isn't quite the limit of it. I don't hold a brief for the effort that was made last year to put on *The Hidden King*. This is a poetic drama.

BROOKS: Mr. Starr has something he wants to—

STARR: Bill, let's get back to Don Davidson's dilemma. And I think it is really Don Davidson's dilemma. He's posed a very interesting problem here, and we've talked all around it without getting at the guts of it, it seems to me. First, has poetry reached a kind of ultimate sterility, the point of no return, because it's no longer oral, or bardic? And why is that true? Now there may be several reasons why that kind of poetry is not in order. But I want to rule out immediately Don's suggestion that it's because of the *zeitgeist;* the temper of the times is against it. That isn't good enough. One of two things must be true; and it seems to me—as Bill Elliott has suggested—that there isn't a big enough poet— and by big enough, I mean objective enough, godlike enough, emotionless enough—to describe it. And there may be a much more sinister reason, too, if Don will permit me. You see, a great epic poem, or any great truth, or any myth, has to be true—has to be true anthropologically. And may-

be the frustration that comes from and through this inability to describe our civilization comes from the fact—I'm
only posing this as a possibility—that we're on the wrong
side. Maybe what we want to say is completely untrue. We
may be swimming against the stream that is the real stream
of the future, "the wave of the future," if you will let me
use a corrupt phrase. Now that's the crux of this matter,
plus the confusion that exists between the poetry that the
Fugitives wrote and a different era entirely—the succeeding
era, which coincided roughly with the great economic depression, the political era of the prose writers, the Agrarians.
I think a sharp separation should be made in our minds—
surely for posterity, if for no other reasons—between these
two things. I know that it's not the temper of the time. The
times are out of joint, certainly; but name one period in the
history of the world when the times weren't out of joint.
You may think of your grandmothers' lives as being calm
and equable, or anybody's grandmothers', or your grandmothers' grandmothers' lives as being calm and undisturbed. It wasn't at all. Maybe we are caught up in our
objections to modernism simply because we don't like
change. We don't like change not only from what we used
to know and used to have, but we don't like change from an
ideal that we wish we had, maybe an ideal that never existed
at all. Now these are pretty terrible thoughts I am trying
to express. But they may be terribly important in evaluating poetry and particularly modern poetry. Maybe we need
a great epic poet who can evaluate the enormous changes
that are happening today—the speeding up, the mechanization, the Leviathan that's crushing us all—and rise above
it and give us the real truths that will survive. This isn't
the end of the world; it's just another era, that's all.

TATE: Well, Alfred,— You go ahead, Don. [*laughter, and
general murmur*]

ELLIOTT: Well, you really stirred the animals up that time.
[*laughter*]

DAVIDSON: I'd like to say—

STARR: And I meant to.

STEVENSON: It didn't work for Hart Crane.

DAVIDSON: May I start first?

BROOKS: By all means, go ahead, Don. Please.

DAVIDSON: Those are perfectly familiar arguments, Alfred. I hear them all the time.

STARR: Oh, [*laughing*] I'm sorry.

DAVIDSON: They are mistaken in the idea that we are objecting to change. You are offering essentially the arguments that are contained in Toynbee's analysis of the disintegrating civilization. He reduces it to a conflict between archaists, who of course don't like change and want to jump backward in the stream of time, and the futurists who want to impose upon the present the pattern of the future that has not yet arrived. And that is what all modernists—and you, I think, are one—argue, you see. Well now, of course, that's not a climate in which the poet can perform because if we have to change every time science changes its immediate working hypothesis, then we can't produce any poetry at all.

STARR: The truths of poetry never change, Don. They are immutable. All we need is that godlike lack of partisanship that can evaluate it. That's all we need. [*amidst general murmuring from Davidson and Tate*]

TATE: This discussion has become much too highfalutin, much too highfalutin. [*laughter*]

ELLIOTT: That's the trouble with metaphysical poets— [*confusion and murmurs*] Whenever you run them into metaphysics, they say it's highfalutin. [*laughter and murmurs*]

STEVENSON: They're absolutely right.

TATE: Well, the little point I had to make was simply that all ages are ages of transition and distress. People are at loggerheads, both inside and outside. But we've got something pretty formidable and something that may be unique in history. We've got constant pressure from all sorts of directions, in this high-powered commercial, technological situation which corrupts the language. Every word that appears in the newspaper or over the radio is debased. Now John Donne's spiritual crises were just as difficult as ours, but the language wasn't as corrupt. He didn't have to invent a language. I think T. S. Eliot said a very nice thing about that. [*murmurs and confusion*] You know he translates a phrase from Mallarmé, "to purify the language of the tribe." That's what every modern poet has got to do, because in the pre-nineteenth-century cultures there wasn't so wide a gap between common speech—the so-called man in the street, or Wordsworth's ideal peasant—and the educated man.

BETHURUM: How do we know?

TATE: Well, because we know.

STARR: You may be underrating the common man now. If you were to speak in your most erudite fashion to an ordinary audience, I think they would understand you perfectly, Allen. We may be doing them and ourselves a grave injustice in underrating the average—

TATE: It isn't a question now of speaking in an erudite way. It's simply that the words in common usage in the ordinary human affairs, day after day, are debased by sociology, commercialism, and what not.

BROOKS: The language is corrupt. I read the newspapers every day; I know it's corrupt. [*laughter*]

ELLIOTT: Of course it's corrupt, but it's always been corrupt—

TATE: No it hasn't, not in the same way, no.

DAVIDSON: [*amidst confusion*] Of course, worse in print than anywhere else.

WARREN: [*amidst confusion*] You go listen to Eisenhower—

LYTLE: Now may I say—

BROOKS: Andrew, yes, by all means.

LYTLE: Going back to your epic. It isn't a question there —I mean, Alec, I don't think it was a simple society at all. It was a very complex society, but what you had was a kind of a ritual that was commonly understood and practiced on that—

STEVENSON: Framework.

LYTLE: —on that, in a kind of maybe a—

TATE: At the moment, Steve, since we use the word *framework*, we are indicating that we don't really believe in it.

STEVENSON: It's not a debased word, Allen, of course.

TATE: We've all used it, you know.

ELLIOTT: Now, but look here. I mean if Andrew Lytle's observation is correct—and I think it is, I think it's a very important one that we ought not to lose sight of—isn't it the poet's job to create ritual? [*murmurs and confusion*] Wait a minute; I know this is absolutely anathema.

TATE: It's just not true.

ELLIOTT: [*to Tate*] My dear boy, you are not in your position of God. [*laughter*] Alfred Starr has said poets must achieve something godlike. And this is—

TATE: Well, you see, I thought that was too highfalutin.

ELLIOTT: I know you said that—

TATE: You're expecting too much of poets—

ELLIOTT: This is precisely the issue that's now joined. I mean, is poetry capable of creating a ritual in society again?

TATE: No.

ELLIOTT: Wait a minute. What is the function of the poet? This is the point that you've really got to ask yourself—

TATE: To write something that people want to read in verse, whether long or short, and whether long or short will depend largely on the talent of the poet and/or the time in which he lives.

ELLIOTT: I don't think this is really quite adequate, because—

TATE: You boys are too highfalutin, that's all. [*murmurs*]

DAVIDSON: I'd like to add another footnote on the epic—

BROOKS: What's this, Don?

DAVIDSON: John mentioned Ker, and Dorothy brought up some matters there. But these nineteenth-century versions of the history of epic and the scholarly interpretations based on them are probably all wrong. And you have only to go back to Homer to realize that they are all wrong; and so I don't think we ought to base anything on what Ker says and all the people like that, because they are working under the analogy of the theory of evolution, you see, which doesn't really apply at all and just has to be discarded.

ELLIOTT: Well—

DAVIDSON: And that's why Andrew's comment on the simple society—you see, the use of that term—is wrong. It's our society at present that is simple, to the point of being a fools' society. And it's the earlier societies—here and there, not all of them—that were much more richly complex than our present society is. So I think that anything based on that particular kind of examination of the historical evidence just won't stand up.

STARR: If it's a fools' society, it's the fault of the wise men who are still alive. [*murmurs and conversation*]

DAVIDSON: Well, we've got a "wise man" in the White House, now, for example—

TATE: This seems to me a little like Archie MacLeish's argument that the poets have let us down. You've got the poets up so high they must run everything, you see.

ELLIOTT: The other argument is like Randall Jarrell's argument that the poet is a poor, abused fellow because he doesn't have an audience. You can turn it either way. Actually, what I want to ask Don to consider—and I think Andrew has suggested it—is this: if you have a function for the poet today, is he capable of making any head against this, or is he in the grip of the wave of the future? Is the wave of the future completely deterministic? Is his choice of symbols and his—Let's take an epic that never has been mentioned here tonight at all, the Arthurian legend. That's a very authentic epic, and Mallory gave it some currency. It was popularized and with considerable effect by Tennyson in the nineteenth century.

BETHURUM: But why do you call it an epic, originally, Bill?

ELLIOTT: Because— You can make all sorts of definitions, Dorothy, but the essential definition of an epic is the testing of a hero by the trials the gods, or circumstance, or fate have put upon him. And he embodies in his own struggle the virtues of the society.

DAVIDSON: I think that's too narrow a definition because there's a vast lot of epical literature, you see, that you really ought to include under the head of the epic; and just because Ker and people like that talk about folk epics and things of that nature, you see—

ELLIOTT: Yes, I'm not trying to go back to folk epics—

DAVIDSON: You shouldn't narrow it down too much—

ELLIOTT: Excuse me, I'm saying that the Tennysonian business, recapturing *Morte d'Arthur,* is in itself an epic of the type I'm talking about. And I think it had a perfectly enormous effect in shaping the concept of nobility, which has gone out of society. Nobility is the thing that the poets have no longer celebrated, because, by example, the ignoble, or the human, are the things that are common to all men—the things that you can explore, if you want to run them to their ultimate conclusions, in Proust, as well as anywhere else.

DAVIDSON: Well, the test of an epic is its general currency, at all levels. And Tennyson's epic—so-called epic—is nothing but a textbook piece, and has only historical interest at that.

ELLIOTT: I would bet you my boots that many a boy who has gone into the air, with his machine guns and whatnot, has been buoyed up by this conception of knightliness, the concept of mission. If Alfred is right about what he said, if the West has no concept of mission any longer, if there is a wave of the future that is in the hands of other people, if Khrushchev and—you see, I have to deal with these: I work on the planning board of the National Security Council, and I do see some of these things close up, as to where they hit our society and what our reactions are; and I admit they are not encouraging. But is it a lack in our society, is it something that we are incapable of formulating? Personally, I believe that there are a great many values in this society that are capable of that formulation. I think Lincoln embodies a very large part of them, and I think he would be capable of being an epic exemplar. When old "A.E.," whom I also sent back for you boys to consider a little bit during the Fugitive period, wrote *The Abattoirs, The Interpreters,* he was trying to do something of this character; and he himself came to your conclusion, that he couldn't do it in a long poem, in an epic. He gave it up, too. But isn't this the dimension of poetry that we've precisely renounced?

BROOKS: Well, Bill Elliott, it seems to me that what you are saying—the turn that conversation's taken here—is that you are demanding that poetry be, or do, what religion once did—

ELLIOTT: Precisely.

BROOKS: —and that's back into the old Matthew Arnold trap.

ELLIOTT: Trap, if you like. [*laughing*] I mean, whose trap?

BROOKS: Well, let's put the matter this way. I'll say my piece shortly, then shut up so that the rest of you— I'm all right; I've got my religion. I think that religion's important, but I think that once you try to make poetry do the work of religion, you've got an *ersatz* religion and an *ersatz* poetry.

ELLIOTT: Is there no connection between them?

BROOKS: Sure, there's a connection.

ELLIOTT: Well, I'm asking to be shown how—

BROOKS: Henry Luce is doing this very thing.

ELLIOTT: No, I don't think so—

BROOKS: Oh, I think he is.

ELLIOTT: I mean you're presenting me with a very *ersatz* piece and asking me to accept it.

BROOKS: Henry Luce and Khrushchev have exactly the same conception of literature.

ELLIOTT: Oh, not really.

BROOKS: Literature must glorify the Soviet Union. Henry Luce trumpets the only good novels are the ones that buck up American morale; the bad novels are the ones that don't.

ELLIOTT: Oh, my dear fellow, this is not the point.

BROOKS: I read *Time* every week— [*laughter*]

ELLIOTT: That's your trouble. You're too full of reading *Time* every week and are reacting against it. [*laughter*] But you haven't yet given us anything in the way of the poet's function to get away from the Henry Luce version into something more genuine.

BROOKS: Don't go to the poets for that.

ELLIOTT: Well, why not?

BROOKS: Because that's not the poet's job.

ELLIOTT: All right, then, define me the poet's job and I'll be content.

BROOKS: The poet's job is to tell the truth.

TATE: It's to write poetry.

BROOKS: All right, but it's a dramatization of man's estate.

ELLIOTT: Oh, I wouldn't be a jesting Pilate and ask you what is truth, and pause not for a reply; I really pause for a reply. You say that Henry Luce is the only kind of truth in our society?

BROOKS: No, but Henry Luce wants poetry to do what you want poetry to do.

ELLIOTT: No! He doesn't at all.

TATE: I think he does, Bill; but you know more about poetry —and you know good poetry.

ELLIOTT: I know more about what the values of this society are.

TATE: Well, you know both.

ELLIOTT: And that's what a poet has to know.

TATE: But I think both of you are the descendants of Matthew Arnold, just as Cleanth said.

RUBIN: Mr. Brooks, may I ask a question?

BROOKS: Certainly, by all means, Mr. Rubin. Go ahead.

RUBIN: Why did none of the Fugitive poets, with all their interest in the Civil War, attempt to write an epic poem about the Civil War?

ELLIOTT: That's a very good question. A very good question. [*murmuring*]

BROOKS: I think they were good enough poets to know that you can't write an epic in this day—

RUBIN: Why didn't they do it?

BROOKS: Well, now, this is foolish to address the thing to me when here is John Ransom, here is Allen Tate, here is Don. Let's move around the circle.

STARR: I suggested two answers to that: one is that they were not big enough poets [*laughter*] and the other is—

RUBIN: I wouldn't say the answer lies quite in that direction.

RANSOM: I don't think that we would get far—whether we get much profit—in deploring our stature as poets. [*laughter and murmurs*] I think Eliot made a tremendous impact on the reception of poetry, the receivers of poetry, just at the time that the Fugitives were going, but that Yeats didn't make his impact on us. I know that his influence was slight—

ELLIOTT: Yes, that's quite right.

RANSOM: —but Yeats was a great hero, and I think what he did might pretty well account for the thing that seems to be desired here. His girl wouldn't accept his love because he was, as he said, a contemplative man and not a primary man. [*laughter*] So he changed his tactics; and even after it was too late to get Maud Gonne, he went ahead and changed his life anyway. [*laughter*] He did his antithesis, which was public affairs. Well now, the Fugitives were very green in public affairs. I certainly can testify to that for myself. I had very little interest in public affairs. Public causes, if they were near to me, I just immediately took out for them and was perfectly satisfied with them. But Ireland seemed to be, in many ways, the liveliest little country in Europe. And certainly there was nothing in America like Ireland, though the South was the most like Ireland. Now, I didn't know then what the politics of my fellow Fugitives was, and

I didn't care; and I supposed that poetry had nothing to do with the paths of politics. But these poets, they learned first the oral part of poetry, and they gave oral effect to their poems. And Yeats became a great prose speaker and the master of an audience. And they had the most delicious problems in Ireland. They had at least two problems: Yeats was very much concerned about "the rise of the masses," to use Unamuno's phrase, and the therefore certain degradation of the general culture to the popular level. But on the other hand, he wanted to see if that was hopeless. The other cause that he was interested in was the freedom of Ireland, and even that didn't affect him much, until Easter, 1916. But eventually he found himself a great public figure on both sides, and the whole Irish public, the whole Irish society of literary men were engaged in it; and that couldn't have come until much later with us. With the Fugitives, it came after we had dissolved as a concert of poets. And so in prose we took off after an ideal society which we knew was a lost cause. And of course now there's a bitterer thing than that which has come up in the South; namely, the problem of desegregation. And so we've got now the most exquisite problems that rest on any country that's at peace, to say the least of it. And I could wish that we had great literary men engaging in it. And they might cut a very great figure. It might be the difference between making a civilization and just going along with a shabby culture. And I would think that it is a wonderful stimulus if we would look at the example of Yeats and his Irish men of letters. But we didn't mature to that point at all as practicing poets. I wish we could now start all over. [*laughter*]

ELLIOTT: Well, Johnny, I thrust it upon you, to the best of my ability. I sent these boys over, and we hobnobbed with them—not as much as you did with Robert Graves and Laura Riding, and some other lesser figures in the world. But the point is that you've given a very fine analysis, it seems to me, of the kind of problems that we did not turn our attention to.

RANSOM: He proved, I think, that he could coarsen his poetry, that he could colloquialize it, that he could give up the ancient, mystic, Gaelic element of language and still could be brilliant and effective.

STARR: To me this is—

RANSOM: And we haven't done that type of poetry.

STARR: —this is the most interesting and significant thing that has been said tonight: that John Ransom, who is a great and enduring lyric poet, has said that he was not interested in public affairs. Isn't that the clue to most of what we've been saying here tonight?

TATE: Are you concerned with the poet's effect on public affairs or what Yeats' interest in public affairs did for his poetry? I should think he had very little lasting effect—

BROOKS: His own testimony was that he had next to no effect on public affairs. [*general conversation and murmurs*]

TATE: And I would disagree with John about one point. I don't think he coarsened his language. By making it more colloquial, in a certain way he actually elevated it. And made it more subtle.

COWAN: Aren't we seeming to underestimate the tremendous effect of this group? The Southern Literary Renaissance, certainly, has been mentioned even in the *London Times Literary Supplement*—

ELLIOTT: [*amidst general murmurs*] That fixed it, that embalms it.

COWAN: —and it seems to me that we can't even estimate the effect that this group had. And so to waste our time—maybe it isn't wasting—but at any rate, to keep saying, "Why didn't we write epic poems?", seems to me rather strange.

TATE: I feel that way, too.

BROOKS: Well, Allen, why didn't you write—

TATE: Why didn't I write an epic poem? I'm too lazy.

RUBIN: Why didn't you write *The Fathers* as an epic poem rather than a novel?

TATE: Because it's not an epic subject. It's too complicated.

DAVIDSON: But he did write—the Confederate veteran addresses his comrades in—I don't remember the title—

TATE: But that isn't an epic poem.

RANSOM: And if your achievement is perfect expression, as *The Fathers* was in prose, why lament that it didn't get some other kind of form?

RUBIN: I'm not doing that at all.

RANSOM: I know, this is a rhetorical question.

DAVIDSON: Well, I can tell you some of the reasons why it's so difficult to write a Confederate epic; there are just obvious difficulties. You can't find a hero that you can use, nor can you invent an adequate one at this time. Any hero you might take won't do for an epic, partly because he's been too well documented. If you want to take Forrest, then if you write a Forrest epical thing—as I did in a fragment—

LYTLE: "The Running of Streight."

DAVIDSON: —why you're competing with Andrew Lytle and Wyeth and Booty Henry and all the rest of the people who have annotated Forrest. And if you—

LYTLE: Don, did you leave out Allen Tated? [*laughter*]

ELLIOTT: [*at the same time*] That's almost as bad as embalming him in the *Sunday Times* in London.

DAVIDSON: Booty Henry annotated him. Then if you take Lee you're up against Freeman, in an epic. But if you take a more lyrical dramatic form, then Freeman has no argument against you.

TATE: I think the point John made a while ago applies here, too. The novel has taken over some of the former duties of poetry, and prose generally has done that.

ELLIOTT: Well, this is an abnegation, abdication.

LYTLE: Well, let me say this, in all humility here, that the poet is the maker now; and—there's no good phrase, but "prose fiction" is I think a bad phrase for the novel, because the novel will last—

RANSOM: The novel is poetic fiction.

LYTLE: Yes, that would be better, because the novel, it seems to me—I don't know what Red would think about this— lies in its point of view and its structure. And of course the structure is not saying much, but it's where the point of view can shift. Now the moment that you can make the mind staid, you see, you can shift the point of view, say, from any area of the consciousness to get different effects. You can get the dreamlike effect, if you slip it over the line. Then you can get in the scene, the epical quality, but you also get the panoramic effect, or the pictorial effect. That is what fiction has added to drama and the scene. And it seems to me now from Flaubert down through James and all, and without going into the Russians at the moment, that you have great possibilities in the use of the point of view that you've never had before in the early nineteenth-century novelists, who were really reduced to the simple art of narrative, like, well, Thackeray and Dickens. They weren't always simple, but that was the basic tone of their fiction. The moment that you put the point of view in the central intelligence, you can do much more than maybe James has done, although I know that's heresy.

THORP: I'd like to ask Mr. Elliott why he objects to the fact, as he seems to here, that some of the Fugitives have written excellent novels.

ELLIOTT: I don't object to it. I think it's merely a confession. I look back on a period of time, since about 1926—roughly a date at which I returned for a visit with the Fugitives, I remember, and got thrown out again because I didn't believe in Agrarianism or the neo-Confederacy as the answer to our problems.

WARREN: Your dates are wrong there.

ELLIOTT: Well, 1930. [*laughter*] What's five years more or less among poets? [*laughter*] But in that period something very interesting happened. Now it's true that some of the practicing poets in the Fugitives went on and produced a volume or two—rather slender—from that time on. But poetry as a medium appeared to be an inadequate vehicle for whatever they were interested in. This is the point that I am concerned with, and I just leave it with you to reflect on. It's not anything that I propose to settle. But it does suggest Alfred Starr's somewhat—

THORP: Well, my point is that the novel, after all, is the great form of our time, and extraordinary things have been done with it, and people right in this room have done extraordinary things with the novel.

ELLIOTT: Of course.

THORP: And why isn't it a good thing that—

ELLIOTT: It is. It isn't what the Fugitives set themselves to do. They began in a very interesting way—[*indistinguishable murmurs and conversation about the fact that nobody, as Tate says, "took an oath" that the Fugitives were going to limit themselves to poetry exclusively. Tate finishes by saying "nobody ever did that."*] No, nobody ever did. But the interesting thing is that poetry ceased to be the vehicle. [*murmurs*]

TATE: Or has it now?

LYTLE: Well, I'm just asking this question. I mean I'm perfectly willing to—

DAVIDSON: Well, we're not dead yet, at any rate. [*laughter and general conversation*]

ELLIOTT: A very interesting question is: How many people, with the exception of Red Warren, have published a volume of verse—except collected verse, and things of that sort—in the last twenty years? [*general murmurs*] Well, there have been stray performances, but they are not sustained business. I mean the Fugitives as a poetic group appeared to have a period, and this is what I'm interested in. I don't know what the reasons for it are.

STARR: Well, I want to suggest again to Mr. Rubin that when the creative artist becomes confused, really confused—not indignant, because he can be a poet and be indignant— but when he becomes confused, angered, and frustrated, then inevitably he must write prose, not poetry. It's that feeling. He can be indignant and write his poems as an objective person who sees the truth and knows it; but once the feeling of frustration gets there—*zeitgeist* sets in—he is reduced to polemics. And polemics are not good in verse.

TATE: [*amidst several speaking at once*] Well, Alfred, would you suggest that literary criticism is a symptom of frustration in poets?

STARR: Well, I don't want to get into Freudian mechanics here. [*Tate and Starr speak indistinguishably at the same time here*]

RUBIN: I don't think anybody who's confused can write anything, really, that's much good, whether he's a fiction writer, or a novelist, or a poet, or—

COWAN: A critic.

RUBIN: —a critic.

RANSOM: He may be confused chronically, but he has acute periods of insight.

TATE: Yes,—[*general conversation*]

THORP: I've been more curious about their not writing satire, than epics.

BROOKS: What's this, Willard? Would you say it again?

THORP: Another question to ask here is why didn't the Fugitives write satire? [*general conversation*]

WILLS: We did a little bit—

RANSOM: There's a lot of satire in Don.

BROOKS: But obviously not much more satire than epic, and I should think for the same reason: that satire involves a definite, accepted community of belief almost as much as epic does, not quite.

THORP: There is also the condition that you are in some revolt against the society.

BROOKS: Yes.

RANSOM: This starts with the sense that your auditors are against you and you've got to win them.

COWAN: But there's a stand against which you are pleaders.

BROOKS: Exactly, yes.

DAVIDSON: I think the moderator ought to call on Merrill. He hasn't said a word.

BROOKS: I think we should, too. Merrill, remedy this defect immediately. [*adjusting the microphone*] I'll hold this thing still.

MOORE: Well, I can ask only a dialectic question, and that is I'd like to go back to the—not to divert the talk—but I'd like to go back to the definition of the epic which I feel has not been satisfactorily expressed. I assume that everyone is assuming that *The Iliad* and *The Odyssey* are true epics, and I assume from what Mr. Tate said—what Allen said— that *The Aeneid* is a synthetic, or non-oral, epic; but I don't think we've come to any real agreement about the epic. We are talking about the emperor's clothes, as far as I am concerned. And I'd like to ask Mr. Ransom if *The Dynasts*, written in the last century, would fit under any given application or definition of an epic?

RANSOM: Well, I feel that the word fantasy—and I would make that a very noble term and let it cover a lot—and I would think that that was a fantasy rather than an epic. It certainly didn't intend to be a factual account, and it sort of sublimated the comment into a mythology of commentators, of spirits talking.

MOORE: Well, that would apply to Vergil also, wouldn't it, Allen?

TATE: I don't think so. I think John points to a very great difference between a poem like *The Dynasts* and even *The Aeneid*. *The Aeneid* is based pretty firmly on the Homeric epical belief. *The Iliad*—

MOORE: We are really talking about epics. Are we talking about Homer?

TATE: I think what we are really talking about is the Platonic archetype which doesn't exist in literature at all. [*laughter*] Don't you think so, Dorothy?

BETHURUM: Yes, I think Homer was as aristocratic and non-popular, probably, as you could find.

DAVIDSON: Well, there wasn't anybody that claimed it was popular, in the sense we are talking about.

BETHURUM: No.

TATE: No, that is quite true.

DAVIDSON: That's Ker's error, and people like that. I don't mean him necessarily—

BETHURUM: Yes.

DAVIDSON: —but people of that sort.

MOORE: Well, what are we talking about? I'm—[*laughter*]

TATE: Well, I think Bill Elliott over here has been indulging in what Dr. Sanborn* used to tell us was the fallacy of reification. [*laughter*] We've got a literary genre erected into a Platonic idea. And the genre—

COWAN: —doesn't really apply to anything.

TATE: —doesn't really exist except in its particular examples and its mutations, and by the time you examine all the mutations, then what happens to the genre? It begins to disappear.

MOORE: Well, now, I'm used to listening to people eight hours a day, and I'm trying to construct in my mind, or reconcile, three theories, or theorems, that have been proposed, one by Bill Elliott, one earlier by Don, and one by Alfred. But I got the distinct impression that just when we were beginning to get this concept formed that you, Allen, pulled it apart by *reductio ad absurdum,* by saying that this is all getting too "highfalutin."

TATE: Yes.

TATE: Getting too Platonic. Too big.

MOORE: I'd like to hear you explain your meaning of "highfalutin." And that's what you are doing when you say something—

TATE: Well, now, I think Cleanth made me think of it a minute ago when he said that Bill—

COWAN: The poet must be verified.

TATE: —and Alfred were expecting the poet to give us a religion.

COWAN: Yes.

TATE: Something like that.

MOORE: Well, now—

* Herbert C., Professor of Philosophy at Vanderbilt.

TATE: I think the poet gives us the highest form of amusement, and it's connected with—

STARR: No, women do.

TATE: No, no. Well, the highest form of amusement of which literature is capable.

ELLIOTT: People look in different directions.

WARREN: That's the highest form of *be*musement you may have. [*laughter*]

ELLIOTT: Well, Allen, I'd like to offer just a comment or two to straighten out this bemusement, or the highest form of amusement. People look in very different directions for this, but surely poetry is, in its essence, symbolism, isn't it?

TATE: Why is it?

ELLIOTT: Well, I don't know. I mean I—This is again an effort at getting some kind of a groundwork that Merrill has asked for.

TATE: Well, there are symbols in lots of poetry.

ELLIOTT: Well, all right, but I mean if poets do not create symbols that have a validity in the society, they have to take the symbols from the society; they have to have some currency. This has been one of the common grounds—the few common grounds—that we have been proceeding on. Sometimes the society seems to be out of joint to the degree that symbols are not viable, in that awful word that's passed around. They are just not understood, and they are not common currency. And the usual complaint of poets in our time is that there's no tradition. I remember hearing Johnny elaborate this at great length and very convincingly: that the poet's job was a hopeless job, because he hadn't some background that was sufficiently common to be currency for everybody concerned. My suggestion is that the mythology that poets deal with is a universal kind of mythology. It's picked up from all sorts of past epics. I really ask you this question: Can you think of any really mature culture—I don't know the Chinese well enough to test it out, and somebody suggested to me that people who don't take dairy products don't have epics; this is one of the things [*laughter*] that is connected with the bovine business; I'm not prepared to explore that—but I'm just asking you can you think of any culture in the world that has not been shaped by a series of symbols of what were the heroic virtues that were to be imitated in the society?

TATE: It strikes me as rather curious, Bill, that in all this discussion Christianity has not been mentioned.

ELLIOTT: I'm prepared to allude to it.

TATE: Is that a myth or not; or do we want to discuss it?

ELLIOTT: In these terms it is, yes. It's a *mythos* in the Platonic sense.

TATE: Yes, that's true.

ELLIOTT: It's a way of life which is symbolized and which has a definite inner connection of symbolisms in a myth, a *mythos*. And that *mythos* is in the epic form, personified, I would suggest, and that poets—

TATE: Well, now we've had *The Divine Comedy* and *Paradise Lost* as the great examples.

RANSOM: We've had Herbert, and—

ELLIOTT: [*amidst murmurs*] Heavens, we've got all kinds of epics if you want to talk about them in other languages, too. I mean there are a number of epics; I suppose the *Cid* is in a certain form a kind of a curious epic. But—

TATE: If we're looking for an epic to give us the religion of—

ELLIOTT: The Finnish epics, the Norse epics, the things that Wagner took his inspiration from in the Germanic epics. These are common ground; the—

TATE: I had—

ELLIOTT: The Parsifal story is an epic that is interlinked throughout all these other things. These are the symbols which cultures have been based upon in the education—in the *paideia* sense of the Greek education—that shape the values of the society.

STARR: Because they are true.

ELLIOTT: Well, I'm not passing judgment on that. They are true in the sense that they satisfy the basic needs of the society.

COWAN: But do they really shape the values of the society, or do they not reflect the values?

ELLIOTT: My dear girl, I don't know how you're going to disentangle those two elements, but they certainly do both.

COWAN: I didn't mean—

TATE: But Bill, there's a very difficult point involved here. From the point of view of the Homeric heroes, at the time they presumably were fighting at Troy, the Greek mythologies represented in *The Iliad* would have seemed to them very decadent. You see, it wasn't the Greek religion that involved them; it was a stylized mythology, very much so, made humanistic.

ELLIOTT: You and I both studied under Dr. Tolman,* and I spent some years at Oxford later on pursuing some of these subjects, and I think this is a very moot point. I don't think you can say that the culture of Athens, for instance, did not have a very definite relationship to both Apollonic and to Pallas Athena, and that Greek culture had the common Apollonic tradition that the Delphic and Phidian— You can go through this and document it.

DAVIDSON: That's partly true, but—

* Herbert C., Professor of Greek at Vanderbilt.

TATE: But we're talking about two things; we're talking about—

ELLIOTT: But we're talking about Homer, and we get back to Homer as the sole type of epic. This is, I think, the point that Merrill has raised. Epics have all sorts of characteristics. Our brother Sidney Hirsch, who is absent tonight, gave us some very extraordinary epics; if my memory is correct. "The Fugitive Blacksmith" was the first mention of fugitives that I can think of in a poem, and it was a whole kind of an epic out of the peculiar concoctions that Sidney was trying to create as a poet. Now, he didn't create this to the extent of doing anything—

TATE: I think they were pretty bad, you know. [laughter]

ELLIOTT: Well, I know. You didn't go along with this. It had some impact on Johnny. He wrote a book called *God Without Thunder,* which was somewhat a reflection—

TATE: It wasn't written the way Sidney wrote his epics. [laughter]

ELLIOTT: True enough. Perfectly true; and you rejected this all the way through, Allen.

TATE: I didn't reject it. I just didn't pay any attention to it. [laughter]

ELLIOTT: Exactly. This is a form of rejection. But if you are concerned with them, do you find in Christianity an epic that you can embody in any kind of symbolic form? It has been embodied.

TATE: I can't find in Christianity an epic at all. You don't need to find one. Why can't we just settle for an empirical view of this whole matter? Epics have been written at certain times, in certain nations, in certain stages of culture. They are not written now. And put a period. That's all. Why go from there?

ELLIOTT: Well, if you ask me why we can't settle for an

empirical form of this, I would suggest to you that this is the very basis of our discussion. The empirical is not a way of finding the essence of any metaphysical problem. It's—

TATE: The epic is not a metaphysical problem. It's an historical problem.

ELLIOTT: Excuse me. I suggest to you that it's an effort to connect cosmogony, the gods, the state of the relation of nature to human nature—this is the very essence of the epic, and it is a metaphysical problem in its essence.

BETHURUM: Well, Bill, the same thing is true of tragedy. I mean it appears, it appeared, well, twice, say. And then it never has been written again.

ELLIOTT: Oh, but my dear lady, this is not a disproof of anything that I have said—

BETHURUM: No, it isn't, but I mean—

ELLIOTT: —it is just simply the fact that in the—

TATE: We don't *will* works of literature—

COWAN: No.

TATE: —into existence. You don't—

BETHURUM: And that's it—

ELLIOTT: Oh, go to. I'm not advocating the will to believe. I'm advocating simply the examination of a problem of poets.

JACOBS: It seems to me that all through this discussion there is the undercurrent of feeling that the Fugitives should have written an epic, and the Fugitives didn't write an epic, and what was wrong that the Fugitives didn't write epics?

DAVIDSON: But the real question is what to do now; not, what to do then.

TATE: Do the best we can.

BROOKS: The question is, who else has written an epic since Milton, if Milton wrote an epic?

RANSOM: In Plato's time the Homeric epics were not accepted by the intellectuals—

ELLIOTT: That's right.

RANSOM: —and then it's Homer who is the cause of the rejection of the poets from *The Republic*. And people might have been saying, "Why don't we get some more epics?" But clearly, there's been a sort of reflection on epics and epical situations and epical necessities, and the poets don't want to do that. It goes back to an earlier period. So there were no more epics.

DAVIDSON: I think that's partly mechanical though, John; because it's obvious, you see, that the epic is intended for oral performance and oral currency. And it's obvious that prose fiction is intended for the book and has taken the place of the epic. It seems to me you just can't get away from that. It's partly a mechanical condition of our present age; and if the culture of the book does wane and finally disappear, then you are going to have something else. And I'll venture to make no predictions.

TATE: You'd have something that nobody in this room would like.

RANSOM: Well, doesn't that mean that you have a simpler intellectual order in the oral work, than you must have in the written work?

TATE: Yes.

RANSOM: And that writing and perhaps printing condemns epics to some extent?

DAVIDSON: It's simpler in its technique, John, but not simpler in its totality.

BETHURUM: If printing hadn't been invented, you might have got Robin Hood as an epic hero.

DAVIDSON: Possibly.

BETHURUM: Got all the ballads brought together.

DAVIDSON: Possibly. The ballad—

BROOKS: We've got enough.

BETHURUM: [*amidst laughter*] Yes, we've got enough.

DAVIDSON: The ballads are all you have of the epic tradition in English that is actually current. The ballads do belong to the epic tradition, generally speaking. But they are all that we have that is actually current in our culture at present. It's really there, to a waning extent, but it's still there.

LYTLE: You know it's a curious thing, but you get a true epic sense—I don't know whether you know this novel; it's about the Norman Conquest, called *The Golden Warrior*, by Miss Hope Muntz, but you almost get it there, finally; it's fictional. Do you know that book? Its tone, the epical tone, which comes through—[*indistinguishable murmurs by Tate*]

ELLIOTT: Well, let's—

DAVIDSON: More saga than epic.

ELLIOTT: —let's dismiss this business which I raised about the epic and say that we've said all that we care to say, or that we feel able to say, and with the assistance of our critics have buried it.

RANSOM: I'd like to—

ELLIOTT: Now, what is the function of poetry in the Fugitive group? Is it pure poetry? Is it—

WARREN: Take off the last part of that.

TATE: [*amidst general murmurs*] Now, Bill, I want to get this down on a lower level. I think the function of the poets of the Fugitive group is just to do the best they can.

ELLIOTT: Well, undoubtedly, I mean—

TATE: Given what they've been given, whatever dowry they have—

ELLIOTT: —this is not novel to the Fugitives, is it?

DAVIDSON: Well, at any rate it's given us a subject for discussion.

BETHURUM: [laughing] Yes.

STARR: But you said to provide the highest form of amusement, or the delight for whom? For the reader—

TATE: It is the highest form of amusement in words.

STARR: For whom? For the people—

TATE: For the people that are capable of a high form of amusement.

STARR: Well, that's a very small audience by your own definition. You know I think—

TATE: Well, it's always been small.

STARR: No, now wait—

TATE: It's always been very small.

STARR: I think, Allen, that you half cynically and half in joke are denying standards of all kinds.

TATE: Oh?

STARR: You are denying the real criterion against being measured.

TATE: Well, that's interesting, that surely is—

STARR: Well, what is the function of the poem, Bill Elliott has asked, of the poet? I say it is—the poet is a mythmaker. And what sort of mythmaker?

TATE: Yes, we've got a real division here, a party line.

STARR: No, now wait—just a minute. He makes a myth that is really acceptable. That's what I mean by true—historically, racially historically acceptable to all of us—whether in our subconscious or conscious.

TATE: He may give it a certain form or shape. It isn't invented, you know. It may develop—

LYTLE: You can't make a myth. I mean, you accept it and have it, don't you?

COWAN: [*at the same time*] You can't. You can't.

BROOKS: [*amidst general talking*] I think that a friend of mine has made the most hair-raising pronouncement on this subject. It's really the *reductio ad absurdum*. He's a man that some of you may know—James K. Feibleman, of New Orleans. He's written a couple of books, and in a recent book called *Aesthetics* he says this: We don't have, our poets don't have, the great myths that Greece had—the myths that Aeschylus and Sophocles used. But, he says, we do have the "myth of the year god," and we know more about myth than any other people ever have. We have all our anthropologists. Therefore we will beat the fifth-century Grecian dramas. Well, that to me is a complete misreading—

BETHURUM: Yes.

BROOKS: [*amidst general confusion and conversation*] —all aired by a whole bunch of anthropologists. The poets now can go ahead and beat Sophocles—

DAVIDSON: You have only to read the recent memoir issued —the symposium on myths—by The American Folklore Society to see the proof of what you say.

BROOKS: Yes.

DAVIDSON: And I recommend that you get that—

BROOKS: I certainly shall.

DAVIDSON: —and read it if you haven't seen it, because it

shows you that the people that are writing about myths don't believe in them, and therefore, they can't be written about.

BROOKS: Exactly—

DAVIDSON: They are only interested in recording them and discrediting them.

BROOKS: We've had, of course, a whole rash of books about myths recently—

DAVIDSON: And all of them are absurd.

BROOKS: —by James Campbell, by Richard Chase, a series of articles—

TATE: The best one is by a German, Eric Neumann. He's a comparative mythologist.

BROOKS: The point is, how can you make a balloon go up that has already been punctured?

DAVIDSON: That's right.

ELLIOTT: Yes. This is a very interesting point, that there's no balloon any more.

STARR: Yes, and Allen is holding fast to the myth of Sisyphus. That's probably the only one he believes in.

TATE: Well, yes, I believe I would have to believe in that one among several others. [*laughter*] But Alfred, I hate to be so empirical about all of this, but let's think for a moment of a modern poet who tried to create a myth of America: Hart Crane, *The Bridge*. It ends in practically nothing, goes absolutely to pieces.

DAVIDSON: The same thing is true of Whitman—

TATE: Yes.

STARR: But his life personified that also.

TATE: Well, now, we're just moving into words.

DAVIDSON: He jumped off the steamboat.

TATE: Yes.

WARREN: Well, both of them wrote an awful lot of good poetry on the way—

TATE: They wrote a lot of good poetry on the way. Now— [*general indistinguishable conversation*]

WARREN: —dealt with values, human values on the way.

ELLIOTT: Yes, well let's just talk about those values of poetry that are not connected with the other things for a change. I mean, I think now is the time for you boys to say what is good poetry, what gives you the highest form of amusement.

DAVIDSON: That's much more difficult than how to do an epic.

TATE: [*at the same time*] Well, we'd have to be empirical again. Just name the poets and the poems. [*laughter*]

DAVIDSON: Let's have them turn off the tape recorder now. [*laughter*]

RANSOM: That question never came up in the Fugitives.

TATE: No, I think that was being—

RANSOM: No programming of the poetry.

ELLIOTT: No.

DAVIDSON: No, we talked about technical effects more than anything else.

ELLIOTT: That's right. And we took them by the kind of osmosis that was natural and current. You were the most considerable wise man among us, and we were very imitative, Johnny. I think that's—

RANSOM: No, I don't think that's it at all; we were a group

of very stubborn individuals that couldn't be coerced, if anyone had tried. I don't think that's—

ELLIOTT: Nevertheless the tone of the Fugitives reflects, in a very extraordinary degree, a kind of a wryness and humor and wisdom and detachment that you put on it. Allen's first poem that he showed to me wound up with "he hacked his bones." I remember that [*laughter*]—

TATE: Why bring that up now? [*laughter*]

ELLIOTT: Well, I'm just thinking of the highest form of amusement on this. [*laughter*] I'm really amused—

TATE: That's a rather low form of amusement.

ELLIOTT: But what is the contribution that the Fugitives can give to the concept of good poetry? This is the— [*general conversation and indistinguishable remarks by Tate, Davidson, and Cowan*]

TATE: It's by writing it.

BROOKS: Let's hear Mrs. Cowan on that subject.

COWAN: Well, it seems to me that the brief period of Fugitive poetry—and I think it had, by its very nature, to be brief —discovered, or uncovered, a language, and a set of values that then later in criticism and in fiction has had a tremendous influence upon the whole nation, particularly upon the South. And so I would like, for one, to—if all this discussion about the epic was to make the charge that Fugitive poetry ended in failure, that it was not connected with life and with public affairs—I wanted to dissent with that; because it seems to me that it did have a tremendous effect.

STARR: But you're leaving out what may live forever in this group; and that is "The Lover," in *Poems About God*. You're leaving out "Janet Waking"—

ELLIOTT: And "Captain Carpenter."

STARR: Yes.

BROOKS: [*amidst conversation*] We're not leaving them out—

STARR: Oh yes you are, because this was written by a man who says at the time that he had no interest in public affairs.

COWAN: But what he—

STARR: And these are deathless lyrics, I submit. Great poetry.

BROOKS: What he did is what counts, not what he said.

ELLIOTT: Let's find out why it counts—

BROOKS: John, it's up to you to defend your—

RANSOM: I don't think there's anything to defend there. I have nothing to reply to people who say, "Why don't you write more poetry?" Well, I say, my talent was a modest one, and I did the best I could; and I frequently threaten to do a little more; but I don't like to be held to any concept of magnitude or dimension. And every poet is a law to himself in those matters. But we did not make a program, nor swear any oaths, nor undertake any Herculean labors.

STARR: Nor undertake the solution of political problems.

RANSOM: No. That never entered into our conversation.

STARR: I'm glad to get that on the record.

RANSOM: So far as I can recall. Never.

BROOKS: I think that it becomes my painful duty to make at least this comment, though it need not be a binding one: if we were all a little younger, we would just go on and on and on, and then get up with a lark in the morning. But the longer we go tonight, the more we chop off, probably, tomorrow. I certainly would hate to feel that I was the person who was stopping this perfectly delightful conversation. I hope that our engineers may secretly keep the tape going. But I think it may be the part of prudence, regarding my years and the years of some of you around, if we perhaps subsided at this point. Let me, in saying that, make this comment. Obviously in asking about the epic—I think it's proved a fine point to talk about—we haven't been talking about why the Fugitives didn't write an epic in the sense in which fatuous critics talk about why somebody didn't write the great American novel. [*general murmur*] We were pointing at other things and deeper things. Some of those deeper things I think have pretty well been defined—at least, are coming into definition—and might very well constitute the matter of topics to be broached tomorrow. On the other hand, maybe the very best thing that could be done would be for somebody to throw out a perfectly clean new ball in the morning. I think—

TATE: Well, I think the epic did very well. [*laughter*]

BROOKS: It did very well, indeed.

STARR: May I ask one indulgence of Cleanth Brooks—

BROOKS: By all means.

STARR: —that we may be permitted to expunge from the record his eulogy of Ernest Hemingway. [*laughter*]

BROOKS: Wait a minute! I'm going to demand that the tape keep running until I say this. [*laughter and conversation*] Hold that tiger. This wasn't a eulogy of Ernest Hemingway. I myself don't think too much of *The Old Man and the Sea*. My point was that if you want to look at our civilization and say, "What do all hundred and sixty-five million Americans believe in?," Ernest Hemingway's got about all that most of the hundred and sixty-five million believe in. It's a pretty paltry thing, I'm afraid, but I'm afraid that's a light on—

ELLIOTT: [*amidst general murmurs*] Well, that comment we won't expunge from the record, but just take leave to offer a few minor dissents on it. [*laughter*]

BROOKS: That's all right. Offer all the dissents you like. But don't put me down as bragging on *The Old Man and the Sea.* I think it's one of his poorer novels.

TATE: I do too.

ELLIOTT: Well, we're more pluralistic than that, I think.

BROOKS: Well, now, look, shall we keep the tape running, or is it prudent? [*general murmurs of "yes" and "no," "Don't you dare cut it," etc.*]

JACOBS: Mr. Brooks, now that the tape is cut—I teach Hemingway, and I have this confession to make: that all my students do not go for Hemingway any more. There are some people in this room they go for, but they don't go for Hemingway. Sensibility or something has changed.

STARR: How about Mickey Spillane? [*laughter*]

JACOBS: No, they don't go for Mickey Spillane in the same sense, either.

COWAN: Faulkner?

JACOBS: [*amidst conversation and general confusion*] They go for Faulkner; they go for Warren; they go for Brooks.

SECOND SESSION

Friday Morning, May 4

Moderator: WILLARD THORP

BROOKS: I think it's perhaps time for us to start. I hope that there was not too much clanking of the pump last night. I didn't hear very much. It seems to me that the spring was flowing as it was wont to flow.

ELLIOTT: I thought you were worried about the clinking of the glasses. [*laughter*]

TATE: You're mixing metaphors a little.

BROOKS: Well, that's a different problem. [*laughter*] I wasn't so much worried about that. At any rate, I have asked Willard Thorp whether he would take the moderator's chair. Last night the moderator's chair pretty well disappeared. I hope that it will be a featherbed rather than a chair this morning. I suspect that it will be with all the leads started, all the unfinished business to carry over. At any rate, I'll turn the meeting over to Mr. Thorp.

THORP: Well, Cleanth, this is very flattering for you to ask me to do this. I am certainly unworthy. Perhaps I can say that I represent the great outside audience of readers of the works of the Fugitives over the years and of teachers and critics who have admired them and have watched the extraordinary spread of their influence with delight. It seems to me perhaps that we might begin this morning by asking the people to dredge their memories a bit and talk about the early days, and what went on. I'm sure the record ought to have something about this. It may be that the Fugitives are tired of reminiscing and won't want to, but perhaps we can gently persuade them to do it. I know I have a number of quite direct questions I'd like to ask for the sake of—

BROOKS: Why don't you put some of those questions directly, Willard?

THORP: —and I'm sure that others here will have them. Well, I think first Louis Rubin has something he wants to ask.

RUBIN: Well, I just had a direct question which I thought might start things along this track. I want to ask Mr. Ransom whether he thinks that his poetry would have been the same, if he would have written the poetry he did, if he had not been at Vanderbilt with the Fugitives from 1920 to 1925?

RANSOM: Well, no, I think that I got more from the group than anyone else, because I started a little further back than anyone. I had just done a little book,* which is now extinct, I am happy to say—

TATE: Not quite, John. [*laughter*]

RANSOM: Yes. And if some archaeologist would compare that book with the following book, he would see a tremendous advance; by no means a complete progress, but a great advance. And I am sure that in a group the tone tends to be that of the best people, the most advanced people. Allen Tate introduced me to both the prose writings and the verse of T. S. Eliot. He was much more advanced than anyone in the group. I was not even advanced in the old kind of poetry in English, because I was a homemade English scholar, and my preparation was not for teaching

* *Poems About God* (1919).

English at all; and so there was a crudeness and greenness about my work that needed just what I got in the Fugitive group where everything there was open to a minute and very honest inspection. And so I think more than almost anyone in the group it helped me along wonderfully, and I know it saved many painful years for me in such little progress as I was capable of making.

TATE: Louis, may I suggest another question that you ask John? Ask John if he remembers the first poem he wrote in what we call his characteristic style—the style by which people know him—after the *Poems About God*. I wonder if he remembers that. I think I do. I think I remember the exact moment you showed me the manuscript in Science Hall one day.

RANSOM: I'm not sure, but you told me, Allen, a few years ago; and it's been responsible for my having read the poem in public once or twice [*laughter*] with that remark that you didn't know whether it was worth staying on with Ransom. And you already had seen New York and had been an independent—

TATE: No, I hadn't been in New York by that time. No.

RANSOM: Well, you knew New York, and you had the role of an independent, and you proposed to make a profession of letters. Well, you said it was a poem called "Necrological"—

TATE: Yes, that's the way I remember it.

RANSOM: —which made you think that perhaps I had some promise, that you wanted to— [*laughter*]

TATE: I'm sure that explains it. That's why I stayed on. [*laughter*]

THORP: Well, I suggest that perhaps it might be a good thing if we got a sort of confession from all the members of the group: Why was it that they found the group so congenial, what in particular helped them, encouraged them?

RANSOM: In those days there was no training for a young poet such as is widespread now. It was all homemade at that time. There was no encouragement in colleges.

STARR: That might have been an advantage.

RANSOM: Might have been.

THORP: But, for instance, what about Bill Elliott, who finally headed in another direction? What did he find in the group?

ELLIOTT: Well, I suppose I was as early a practicing poet as anybody in here, for that matter; and I still practice poetry in my secret moments, and have found it very useful just to do it for my own edification, if nobody else's. I suppose probably I practice it more than some other members of the group. But the poems that I showed Johnny may well have touched him off to write a poem called "Necrological," because I wrote some very crude poems on the usual theme of young poets, about death, and so on, and wind and the leaves, that kind of thing. Johnny showed me the first poem I think that he wrote, and it was a departure from his usual modesty and a great tribute to his friendship for me. It was called "The Lover," in *Poems About God.* And "Noonday Grace" and some of the others he wrote of that early group. I think probably we prodded him into correcting our crudities by showing them to him. Allen certainly exposed him to T. S. Eliot, but when he says that he was not acquainted with poetry, he was acquainted with the best body of poetry that I know—

TATE: That's correct, John. We can't let you get away with that.

ELLIOTT: —the classics; and no one who went through *Beowulf* with Johnny, or listened to him expound *Hamlet,* or read some of Shakespeare with that restraint that was so unusual for students of Eddie Mims [*laughter*]—it was a double impact—could fail to say that his unusually modest statement, or characteristically modest statement, was an understatement completely. I mean, he had a very right critical sense marked by that kind of detachment and somewhat courtly wit, that was a refreshing and rare thing in the sentimentality with which we were bathed at that time.

RUBIN: Which one of you is it who wrote—who made the remark that the favorite word of the Fugitives was "escheat"; somebody wrote that.

LYTLE: That's Jarrell, Jarrell.

TATE: I'm to blame for that, Louis. Nobody else. No other Fugitive used it.

ELLIOTT: What was the favorite word?

TATE: The word was "escheat."

RUBIN: Well, somebody wrote this; I don't believe it was Jarrell, was it?

THORP: Well, Louise Cowan ought to know about that.

COWAN: Well, one of the remarkable things about this group, as a group, it seems to me, is the fact that it did meet for so many years before the poetry was written, continued to meet after the poetry was being written—that it held together, which is a rather rare phenomenon. And I would like to hear some remarks about, oh, the relationship of the South to this group. For instance, did a tradition of talk— do you think that had anything to do with it; the feeling that talk was not a waste of time, but a valuable enterprise? Did a feeling of mutual trust, and of what I like to call *gentilesse*—did it permeate the group, and was it responsible for the harmony which existed among such diverging points of view?

ELLIOTT: Well, let me just finish out what I aimed at by commenting on that. When I spoke about Johnny's courtly manner, I think I was perhaps giving a little of the hint of the complete fairness and the very, very moving quality of understanding that he brought, which you may call *gentilesse* if you like, or something of that sort. There was a Southern tradition of being able to argue violently and still be very friendly, because we all respected each other. But I think if one really is honest about it, it was the quality of Johnny's moderation, not as a model but as an example—

TATE: I would agree with that, Bill. I remember John used to take something I had written and put his finger on a certain word and say, "Why is that there?" It was done so casually and with great disinterestedness. You see, he had no animus about him; he was detached, and that's how we learned from him.

ELLIOTT: And this was the example, and the model, that I think restrained the more exuberant characters, like me and others, in our exchanges and taught us something. I remember at Oxford I edited verse one year with some other souls, and belonged to a group there like the Fugitives, but who took themselves seriously. There were Robert Graves and some of the other boys. We used to see there all the good poets at the time the Fugitives were just getting underway. I never found any quality in that group, or in any other group that I was associated with—like the California Poets' Guild, and various other people, and those wretched poetry conferences that I've quit giving at Harvard, because I'm about fed up with the poets in this sense—that were stamped with this quality that you are seeking for. Now I think undoubtedly there is something in the South, and there is particularly something in the fact that many of us were kin to each other several generations back. I believe I am a distant kinsman of both Johnny and Andrew. And we have a sense of community that goes far deeper than probably most people have in that kind of sense—the people who grew up in this region and grew up as boys together, like the Starrs grew up with me. And Sidney Hirsch who is not here and who is a very extraordinary character—

think him anyway you like—injected into it a different level: a dimension of mysticism and philosophy which in the earlier days of *The Fugitive*, I think we'd all acknowledge, was one of the most timely bonds among us, before we began axing the poetry of each other. We had done that in the Calumet Club as critics and things of that sort; we hadn't practiced poetry. Now, what that combination is, I think your question is very properly put. All I wanted to do was to start off by capping the stone I had laid, saying that Johnny really set the tone of that. Allen was formerly the most sophisticated member of that group, I suppose, at that time—and may yet be. [*laughter*] But there was a combination of a certain robustness, a fundamental traditionalism which cemented us, and a complete independence for—what Johnny said quite firmly last night—no programming. A complete resistance to anybody programming anything. And yet the impact of this group focusing on things that he more or less led the way on—because he was formally the most accomplished poet I think among us—that did have its shaping effect.

WILLS: I would like to say something in answer to Mrs. Cowan's question, if I get a chance. This may be one of the few times where I feel competent to comment. We must remember the atmosphere in which the Fugitives started. It was right after the First World War. Many of them had come back from the war. The college was full of students who were in the war. I spent my freshman year—part of my freshman year—half in the Army and half out, and half in college. It's significant that while we were in college, there was a revolt against the revival of the R. O. T. C. that came to nothing but created quite a bit of excitement in the papers. There was a sort of atmosphere, not of violent revolt because we weren't politically-minded and didn't know what we were revolting against, but we didn't like regimentation; and there was some reaction from idealism, because Woodrow Wilson was more or less failing and the League of Nations had been abandoned. And also we had heard a lot of talk about the "New South," the South of Henry Grady, the South of industrialism; and even the potential businessmen among us were not particularly enamoured of that. And it was a time when the late H. L. Mencken was the idol of the students. Even Allen, before he found T. S. Eliot, used to carry Mencken around under his arm.

TATE: Yes, that's true, but not Cabell. [*laughter and general murmurs*]

WILLS: And so, while we were not political and we were not violently in revolt, we were moderately or politely in revolt against something. And also I think Nashville had an atmosphere, combined with Vanderbilt and the fact that this particular group of personalities—part students and part instructors—were there, that helped it. Nashville did have some tradition of talk. There have been three literary clubs here that were founded in the 1880's. John belonged to one of them. His wasn't founded that far back, but they brought businessmen and lawyers and people on the campus together to talk; and while Nashville wasn't Bohemian, or particularly worldly-wise, it was a city where everybody knew everybody else at that time—or at least if they didn't know them, knew who they were—and it was reasonably tolerant. And it was a good atmosphere for a thing like this to develop and to keep going. We weren't encouraged too much—we certainly had no such crowds as were present yesterday—but we were treated with a certain measure of respect and consideration and tolerance as we went along. I don't know whether that adds anything to what's been said or not.

LYTLE: I just wondered—I think that's very interesting. I would like to ask one of you—. You know at the moment there, after the First World War, there was a sort of—well, as a matter of fact, the United States really rediscovered Europe then, you know—

WILLS: Yes.

LYTLE: —and the South sort of came into the nation, and it seemed a kind of a release of energies and interests far spread. And then, as it always happens, you finally found yourself back in the old domestic scene, you see. And that would carry you into the Agrarian days; I mean it really came by concrete instance, which was the Dayton trial.

WILLS: Yes.

LYTLE: In the sense of—

BETHURUM: I was going to ask—I was about to ask whether Oxford had any influence on the inception of this movement, if it is a movement, on the beginnings of these things? I seem to feel that it did. I guess John could answer that better than anybody else.

RANSOM: Well, I don't think so. I wouldn't know.

BETHURUM: I think you would underestimate.

RANSOM: I don't think Oxford had a typical presentation through me in any way. I was so green when I went to Oxford, in spite of my B.A. degree from Vanderbilt; and I didn't come out an Oxford man, quite, I think. I think Elliott was more of an Oxford man that I was. I feel that he was. Perhaps I had further to go than he did; and I didn't quite catch up to the Oxford tone completely, at all, I think.

BETHURUM: Well, in my experience as a freshman and a sophomore in your classes, there was something there that was not quite native, some kind of—what shall I say?— brushing away of the conventions, of the superficialities, which I didn't recognize until I knew something about Oxford myself. And then I thought that was it, probably. Some kind of centering.

RANSOM: Well, I took philosophy and classics at Oxford, what they called the "Greats" course, and I'm sure that both of those were in that and probably that's Oxonian; and I don't think the same thing was well represented at Vanderbilt at that time.

BROOKS: Let me break in just to say this: John would not overemphasize the Oxford business, nor would I. I would say this much, however: that there was a continuing man-of-letters tradition there, even a kind of rich amateur tradition, which by-passed pretty much the Germanic seminar business that came over in the 1880's and 1890's. And I think that that would have joined, probably unconsciously through John did join, the tradition of talk, the tradition of the talented amateur here, as opposed to the professionalism of the German seminar.

JACOBS: I would like to ask in that connection whether the Fugitives were aware of T. E. Hulme and what he had said before the Fugitives ceased publication.

RANSOM: I would say that Allen probably was, and I doubt if anyone else among us was.

TATE: It couldn't have been long before publication ceased, because Hulme's *Speculations* appeared in 1924, and the magazine stopped in 1925. But I don't think it had any real influence on us at all.

THORP: I'd like to ask in that connection what particular individuals brought in particular ideas. Of course at that time in America all sorts of things were flooding in from Europe —French symbolism and so on. Was there much talk, in the group, of these new literary movements and new literary figures?

RANSOM: I think we were a little aware of French symbolism. I don't know how much. I think that was in the back of our minds. I think Donald Davidson—we called him "the romantic"—had that eternal strain of poetry more than any of us. And I'm sure that that was very fertile, that it affected all of us. I think he ought to speak.

DAVIDSON: If you want me to speak on that subject, I would have to go back before *The Fugitive*. Like Bill Elliott, I had John as a teacher, and then began to know him as a sort of miraculous thing to me, as a friend and counselor. And in the poems that John wrote, 1914 to 1916, there was certainly not a hint of any foreign influence that I would be able to put my finger on. And no talk of it at all. What impressed me then was that a man that I knew could not only write poems but could get them published. [*laughter*] If I remember, the poems in *Poems About God* began to appear in magazines like *The Independent* of those years; and John did me the honor to read me some of those poems and show me copies that he probably gave you, too, Bill; I don't remember.

COWAN: And that was before the First World War.

DAVIDSON: That was between 1914 and 1916. And, in fact, I think that I remember the occasion. I mentioned it to Louise Cowan, and John will remember it: when—it might have been the first poem of this group; I believe it was— John called me out, one day after class, I guess, and said "I've written a poem, and I want to read it to you," or words to that effect. And we came out on the campus and sat down on the grass somewhere there near College Hall, and he read me the poem entitled "Sunset." [*murmurs*] And there's nothing but just pure John Ransom in that, it seemed to me.

RUBIN: How about the Chicago Poets? Had you read those people?

DAVIDSON: Well, my only connection, my only awareness of that would have been through Stanley Johnson, who was my close friend and who was keeping up somewhat with that. I remember when *Spoon River Anthology* came out that he was greatly impressed and got hold of the book somehow and called me up in his room in old Wesley Hall and said "Look here, Don, this man has done it. This is what we ought to have done, but he has done it first." And he was greatly chagrined that he had not thought of doing something like that. Stanley Johnson is an important, stern, and sober influence that should not be underestimated in this period. He was very philosophical, and when Dr. Mims in his Nineteenth-Century course in literature would call on the students sometime in the spring of the year to write their spiritual autobiography—he continued that for years and years—Stanley wrote his religious beliefs, which turned out to be his restatement of Bowne's Personalism, which I think he got from Dr. Sanborn. Isn't that right, Bill? Then when the war broke out, I found myself at Fort Oglethorpe as an officer candidate. John was there, too, and he had a lot of the more recent poems he had written in manuscript. And he either gave me copies, or I copied them somehow. And John will remember that we sat out under the pines at Fort Oglethorpe and he read me a number of those poems, among which was, I think, the one about the swimmer, which of all the group was the one that interested me most, but I couldn't figure out what it meant. And when I was commissioned, then, I carried those poems with me all over France—kept them in a trunk locker, and if they hadn't been burned up in the Wesley Hall * fire, I'd have them still. Then, meanwhile, I married, and I wanted something to read overseas; and I entreated my young wife to send me some poetry. But there were restrictions on packages, and so she picked out—all I had for a while was some little book called *One Hundred Best Poems* that she—. [*laughter*] Very poor stuff. That was about the extent of my reading. Then, finally, somehow or other—I don't know how it was—I got on to the fact that Amy Lowell had published a book called *Tendencies in Modern American Poetry*. And she sent that to me. I had that then in France. I suppose it must have come to me after the Armistice. I had that, and that was my first acquaintance, first real ac-

* Wesley Hall, which housed both students and faculty members on the Vanderbilt campus, was destroyed by fire in 1932.

quaintance, with what you would call the French Symbolist poets. Then I tried while I was in France—I thought I ought to be writing some poetry, and I tried to write some poetry in that vein, and wrote it into a little memorandum book. And when I came back after the war to Vanderbilt, I saw Alec Stevenson, and I took those poems to him and showed them to him. And Alec waved them aside as complete trash, which they were. He said I mustn't do that any more. Now, then, I can't remember that the French Symbolist poets were discussed at any Fugitive meeting that I can recall; and if I learned about them before that time, it would be through Allen and not through John, I believe. And I don't recall giving them any close attention whatever during the period of the publication of *The Fugitive*. I don't recall paying any attention to them at all until I started to teach poetry in classes. And I don't remember their ever coming up in English 9, John; because if I remember, John, in English 9, where various of us studied advanced writing, John generally began his instruction in poetry with Shakespeare—Shakespeare's sonnets, if I remember. Maybe he got into Housman, but I don't remember for sure. John would have to correct me on that. So I think that the French Symbolist influence is a late development, and doesn't really belong in the history of the Fugitive group except as it affected Allen and as Allen affected us. That'd be my notion of it.

ELLIOTT: If I could just add a footnote to that, I think that's very important about Stanley Johnson, who was, I think we would all agree, a very astringent mind and a wonderfully tough and good kind of independent, rugged mind, that could test out things. And he was rather widely acquainted. I'd like to add a footnote to what Jesse said. Some of the people around here like John Wilson had magnificent libraries and kept up with all sorts of things that we browsed in. John was a cousin of mine, and he used to give me the run of it, and I would pass around *Spoon River*

Anthology and things of that sort. The Calumet Club has been mentioned before. That was an unusual group of people. Walter Clyde Curry's influence in that was very considerable. And there were a lot of people in it that sort of dropped out who were very shaping influences at this time, because we read an enormous amount of Russian literature, French literature, and things of that sort.

RUBIN: Did you all see *Poetry* magazine?

ELLIOTT: Yes, we saw that. But the final thing I would like to say about this particular subject is that Alec Stevenson ought to be here, because Alec really was, along with Allen, I suspect, as widely lettered in poetry and had about as good critical appraisal, not only because of his remarkable background—what was his father, Scotsman, Canadian? * But, at any rate, Professor Stevenson was a great Sanskrit scholar, and we had the impact not only of Johnny's classics and the tutorial position—which is the Oxford thing that I would like to put in—but also because his relations with us were those of an absolutely first-class tutor in a very informal, warm, personal sense that went beyond any tutor's relationship to the normal thing. Now Alec added to that, to my mind, a very, very important dimension; and I think we'd all agree that Alec had an ear for music, next to Don's, about as good as anybody's. He wrote natural lyrics. I think he was one of the greatest losses as a poet, in some ways, in this group. And he was a very, very, sophisticated fellow in the sense of his widespread acquaintance with other languages than our own and with the English tradition which he was deeply steeped in from his family background.

DAVIDSON: I'd like to ask a question. I would like to ask Allen to say whether he read Baudelaire intensively before he got acquainted with Bill Bandy.* *

* A Canadian by birth, J. H. Stevenson was Professor of Old Testament Literature at Vanderbilt.
* * A Vanderbilt student in the 1920's, William T. Bandy is Professor of French at the University of Wisconsin.

TATE: I think I had. And it was through Baudelaire that I began to investigate the symbolists under the suggestion of some of the early writings of Ezra Pound rather than T. S. Eliot.

WARREN: That was in '23, wasn't it?

TATE: Yes.

WARREN: If I remember correctly that's when I began to read them. Because you and Bill started me reading them—

RUBIN: How did you get on to Pound?

TATE: Well, I don't know. I had seen him in *The Little Review* and in *Poetry* magazine and various others—the *Dial,* which began about 1920.

WARREN: I don't remember a time when Pound wasn't read around here.

TATE: The first time we knew each other, which was in 1921—

WARREN: Yes, fall of '21.

TATE: —well, you'd already read Pound, and so had I.

WARREN: Well, I read Pound as a freshman, didn't I? That's '21-'22. And I guess it was the next year, it was '22 or '23, I guess, Baudelaire and some other French poets.

TATE: When we were rooming together, particularly, we used to talk about him.

WARREN: That was in '22-'23.

TATE: But, Red, I wouldn't think that the Symbolist influence accounted for very much in anything that this group wrote. It was somewhere in the background; we were certainly not Symbolist poets. And I think that some of the critics who have tried to place us in that historical perspective are wrong about it.

WARREN: Well, I think you are right about that. I don't think it counted in that sense—

TATE: No.

WARREN: —I mean, I remember—I think in a very indirect way you'd count it.

TATE: Yes.

WARREN: At least for some people. As far as state of mind was concerned about poetry, it was not in terms of direct use of a method. I mean Baudelaire had a very definite effect on some people, say the line anyway—

TATE: Yes, on me, too.

WARREN: Two or three of us, anyway. I think John passed by without—

TATE: John by-passed those, yes. [*laughter*]

RANSOM: Well, I was two years in France fighting the battle in a rear area, instructing in French matériel, and several nice young ladies introduced me to the poetry of the nineteenth century of France, and I came back—

WARREN: I was saying something quite different from that. [*laughter*]

RANSOM: —and I came back with a lot of volumes, and I know that the French Symbolists attracted and perplexed me a great deal. I may not have talked about them, but they were in my consciousness after 1919. Very decidedly.

WARREN: Well, I wasn't thinking of your knowledge of them, or awareness of them. I was thinking simply, well, something in relation to your own poetry.

RANSOM: Well, I think the—

WARREN: And your own state of mind, temperament, as I read it.

RANSOM: They had a great gift of phrasing, and they had a

great boldness of metaphor. And I felt sure that that belonged some way or other in verse; I don't remember any talk of it, but—

WARREN: I remember your talking about it, not only once but on several occasions. But I wasn't thinking of awareness of it in that sense, but something quite different: just a temperamental affinity which I never detected between your work—

TATE: Same time, Red, you know what Edmund Wilson has called the "conversational ironic" thing—

WARREN: Yes.

TATE: Now it seems to me that John developed something of his own which was similar to that but not in the least influenced by it.

WARREN: It was similar, but it's not based on it; it's not influenced by it.

TATE: No, not at all. No.

WARREN: And I remember at that time that John introduced me to Hardy. And I was struck very early with an affinity there—

TATE: Yes.

WARREN: —again no imitation, no modelling, but an affinity of some kind there which I sensed right away. This has no reference to the topic, but I happen to have an anecdote about John's first book of poems. I encountered in California some years ago a man named McClure, who edits the paper at Santa Monica. He owns and edits that paper. Well, he was in France at the same time that John was as a soldier. And when I was living out there, he wrote me a note—I had never met him or knew anything about him—and said, "I am a friend of an old friend of yours. Won't you come to dinner?" So I went to dinner at his house and had a very pleasant evening. And he said that he was walking down the street with John Ransom, who was a good soldierly companion of his during that period, and they went to get the mail at the battery mail distribution. And they got a few letters, and John got a little package. And he opened the little package, and there were two copies of *Poems About God* in it. And he said John hadn't seen the book before, and he opened it and inspected it with composure, and then turned to McClure and said, "I'd like to give you a copy of this." [*laughter*] And McClure treasured this copy; and over the years, he said, along with other later writings of John's, followed his career with delight.

BEATTY: I'd like to ask if the Fugitives ever systematically studied the writings of a given poet, or just read your own?

WARREN: You mean as a group, or as individuals?

BEATTY: Yes; yes, I mean as a group.

TATE: No, not that I remember.

RANSOM: I think it ought to be said, going back to another point, that I was frequently button-holing people and taking them out into the pasture to read my poems, but [*laughter*] I want it understood that they were always people that could give it as well as take it [*laughter*]; I think that's one of the things, really—that was the whole principle of the Fugitives. There wasn't a man there that couldn't give it as well as take it, and that's what he wanted to do. And, in return, we were always ready to take it provided we could give it. And so that was a very natural basis for a group effort.

TATE: Matter of fact, there was a great deal of excitement between meetings. We'd show each other the poems before the meetings. And that year, much later than the time that Bill and the old members of the group were meeting—about the time Red and I were coming on the scene—there was a very great excitement on the campus. We'd meet Merrill Moore, and he'd whip a poem out of his hip pocket, and with barely a suggestion or the least encouragement, he'd ask us to read it right there standing on the campus.

WARREN: Did you say *a* poem? [*laughter*]

TATE: Well, you see, Merrill, instead of revising a poem, would write ten more; and none of us could ever keep up with him.

DAVIDSON: I'd like to ask a question of Allen, something I've thought about without ever having a chance to work it out: the possible influence of his advanced studies in Greek poetry on his own verse. I know you took those advanced courses under Dr. Tolman—

TATE: Pindar and—

DAVIDSON: Pindar, whom I never studied. I have a feeling it would be of some importance, but I wouldn't know what. When I was in prep school at Branham and Hughes, I had three years of Greek there, and in the senior year we read *The Odyssey*; and after we had gone a certain way, every day's lesson was started by the class being required to read the lesson, metrically at sight. So we were able, roughly, to scan and read aloud Homer's hexameters that way; and it may have had some remote influence on me, I don't know; at any rate, some feeling of dignity and movement of great poetry. And I'd like to ask Allen if he would attribute anything in his work to that influence?

TATE: I don't think I could, Don, in anything very tangible.

DAVIDSON: But you made a number of translations.

TATE: Yes, and—

BETHURUM: You made them at the same time you—

TATE: Yes. Those poems like that are so intangible, it's hard to deal with them.

ELLIOTT: But they are very fundamental—

TATE: Yes, true.

ELLIOTT: —it seems to me that's a most interesting question, and starts a real hare. How many of this Fugitive group had both Greek and Latin, as much as three years?

TATE: Most of us did.

ELLIOTT: I think nearly all of us had three or four years. Wouldn't that be right? You had five, I had five, Johnny had more than that, because he had the "Greats" at Oxford —you really had to be able to compose an ode or an epode if you were good at verse, as well as do prose composition. And in Greek, I think that the grace of Greek poetry—we can't underrate Pindar. The influence of that sort of thing is, I think, very fundamental. And I rather wonder if it wouldn't be an amusing thing to do to take a census of it. When I was teaching some of these boys Freshman English, as a colleague of Johnny's before I went to Oxford, I used to try it out, and my impression was that the best people nearly always had had a great deal of Latin, all Latin, and most of them had had Greek—the people who wrote with some grace, and felicity. And I believe that might be a very interesting part of it.

LYTLE: I started to say I had very little Greek, one year. I think this is the thing about that: that both those languages are so hard that they make you look at the word in all its relationships. And you get the rhythm of the whole composition that way better.

STEVENSON: I'll come along and say that I had six years of Latin and five of Greek.

ELLIOTT: Alec, I was begging for you a little while ago.

TATE: I would think the influence of the classics is more subtle in John's poetry than in the work of any of the rest of us.

ELLIOTT: Well, what this all suggests to me, Allen, is that this was not a "made" group by the usual technique of imitation or even osmosis from some other schools. It was a singularly unselfconscious group, and yet one that felt it had roots of its own. And the combination of those roots, which Mrs. Cowan has suggested, in a Southern kind of community or setting (and Jesse Wills has touched this up by the remarks he has made), plus this classic background in Southern education, I think is more important than the content. I went to the Sorbonne, I studied Mallarmé and Baudelaire and a great many other people; and I remember Johnny discussing these things with me with great insight and helpfulness, in 1920-21. Of course, I left and went to Oxford and I don't know what happened, except when I came back on vacation a couple of times after that.

TATE: Bill, you mentioned Southern education in classics. It may amuse you to know that just the other day T. S. Eliot was talking about that to me. And he said, "You may not have had a very large curriculum in the Southern colleges, but it was sound, because you had the Latin, Greek, and mathematics." He said, "At Harvard, where the curriculum had been ruined by my eminent cousin, Charles W. Eliot," he said, "I never got any education until I graduated from Harvard, because it was sort of like a cafeteria: you just took one little thing after another." I think he probably exaggerated the thoroughness of Southern education, but its very conservatism accounts for some of the things that happened to this group.

THORP: I think the question ought to be asked here, again for the record, who were the people on the faculty that were particularly influential? What were the courses that may have been influential? What were the courses that were cordially disliked, and perhaps by rejection had something to do with the firmness of the group?

ELLIOTT: Well, that's a very embarrassing question.

TATE: Yes it is. Perhaps if we call names—

COWAN: Well, I would like to hear about—

BROOKS: [to Tate] That's what you are here for.

COWAN: —Professor Sanborn, for instance; because every Fugitive with whom I spoke seemed to ascribe to Dr. Sanborn's classes a very great intellectual stimulation. And I wonder if anyone cares to—

TATE: I suppose, John, you were before Sanborn's time, weren't you? Well, did you have—

ELLIOTT: John, tell them the story about your first interview with your philosophy tutor at Oxford. It's too good not to be repeated for the record, I think.

RANSOM: Well, I'll tell it on your responsibility. I don't know whether it's worth the time or not. But when I got to Oxford—

ELLIOTT: We'll get to Sanborn after this, but this was Denny, wasn't it?

RANSOM: —I'd had Collins Denny* in philosophy, and so I appeared to my appointment—the students had individual appointments, at the beginning of the term, to march down the great hall to meet the Dean of the College who would then shift you to your tutors. I was shifted about to five people altogether, and each one of them raised the question of whether I ought to take "Greats," or understood what I was trying. And I was very confident, and I finally got to my philosophy tutor who was a very eminent philosopher named Blount. And he said, "Have you read any philosophy?" And I said, "Yes, I had two years of philosophy at college." "What did you take?" And I said, "We took a course in deductive logic—Aristotelian logic." And he said, "Whom did you read?" And I said, "We had a book by Noah K. Davis." And he said, "Ah, I don't know that name; but did you take anything else?" And I said, "Well, we had a course in inductive logic." And he said, "What did you read?" And I said, "We had a book by Noah K. Davis."

* Professor of Philosophy at Vanderbilt.

[*laughter*] And he said, "A most ubiquitous man." [*laughter*] And then he said, "Did you take any other courses?" I said, "Yes, then we had a course in ethics." And he said, "Whom did you read? But please don't say Noah K. Davis." [*laughter*] I said, "Noah K. Davis." [*laughter*] And he said, "My education is faulty. I don't know Noah K. Davis. But did you take any other courses?" I said, "Yes, then we had a course in psychology." And he said, "I can't bear it, but I feel that you had Noah K. Davis." I said, "Yes." [*laughter*] And it was perfectly true that we had had Noah K. Davis, and no other philosopher, living or dead. [*laughter*] And so he said, "Come to my rooms next Thursday evening at eight, and bring me an essay entitled 'What Is Thought?'." [*laughter*]

RUBIN: Well, who was Noah K. Davis? I'm intrigued.

RANSOM: He was a professor at the University of Virginia under whom my professor had studied, and who had written all the books. [*laughter*]

ELLIOTT: Well, the purpose of this comment was to show that Sanborn was a revolutionary impact in comparison with Denny. And surely the personalism of Borden P. Bowne and a certain overlay of Heidelberg, and the History of Philosophy by Max Weber—

TATE: I had that. [*laughter*]

ELLIOTT: —were the classic pieces; and you did get a very thorough grounding which had the beneficial effect of so irritating you in many ways. In spite of the tremendous learning that Sanborn had, he was so dogmatic that he really provoked all the independent minds into doing some thinking of their own.

TATE: But he never sent us to the library.

ELLIOTT: No, this is true.

TATE: Do you remember that, Dorothy?

BETHURUM: Yes, I do remember—

ELLIOTT: In that he continued a little bit the tradition of Denny, but he had read more books than Denny or he got them at least secondhand, and we were provoked into reading others.

TATE: [*amidst general conversation*] The course in the History of Philosophy was very impressive. I was—

BETHURUM: Oh, it was.

TATE: —terrifically impressive.

RANSOM: And he was a great master of—

WARREN: Didn't he refer to books, though? He'd come to refer to books—

TATE: Oh, yes, he didn't insist that you get them, but—

WARREN: He just kept giving you names and books instead of referring to them—

BETHURUM: [*at the same time*] Yes, yes.

WARREN: —and if you wanted to read them you could go read them.

BETHURUM: I must say that when I went to Yale and took some graduate work in philosophy, I found myself, well, pretty well equipped. That is, there weren't any areas that I hadn't been introduced to, and pretty thoroughly grounded in, really.

TATE: I remember when I was a sophomore, I took Dr. Sanborn's course in Logic. Well, it was the toughest thing I'd ever been up against, because you had to know it letter perfect. It was very, very difficult. There's one more thing. He really liked bad poetry better than good. There was no doubt about that.

ELLIOTT: And it's all the more remarkable, because he was a master of aesthetic theory—. [*general conversation and laughter*] I think this taught us a most valuable lesson, the lack of relationship between the theory of aesthetics—

TATE: Exactly.

ELLIOTT: —and the practice of beauty and art.

BETHURUM: That is one of the best things I learned in college, and couldn't have learned it any way except by example.

TATE: That's right.

RUBIN: Well, how about Nineteenth-Century literature?

TATE: Dr. Mims* presided over that.

RUBIN: I know.

ELLIOTT: Well, now, let's not be harsh about that—

TATE: No.

ELLIOTT: —because Eddie did stimulate a great many people to a certain interest in—I must say that he didn't completely ruin Tennyson for me, and I think most people would have ruined it—

TATE: Well, he made us all read a lot of poetry that otherwise we would not have read.

ELLIOTT: We read a lot of poetry aloud, and he had a great many qualities that were extremely useful.

TATE: And he made us memorize poetry, which was extremely valuable.

RUBIN: What kind of poetry?

TATE: The Romantics and the Victorians, as a rule.

ELLIOTT: Well, after all, there may be others who have so far outgrown them that they don't find them a useful part

* Head of the English Department during his thirty years of tenure at Vanderbilt, Dr. Edwin Mims retired in 1942.

of their education, but I still think rather highly of Tennyson and Browning—

TATE: Oh, I do, too.

ELLIOTT: —as very considerable people.

STARR: Well, today, for example, I can—letter perfect— quote the end of *Ulysses*, those last forty lines, because of Dr. Mims.

WARREN: There are twenty thousand people in Tennessee who can do that. [*laughter*] What are you boasting about?

STARR: It wasn't a boast. [*laughter*]

DAVIDSON: I'd like to add one footnote again there on the philosophy angle. John could have told his tutor at Oxford that in his courses in Greek he had read parts of Plato in the Greek, because we all had to do that. It wasn't presented as philosophy, but we did go through a good part of the *Apology* and some selections from the *Crito* and *Phaedo*, as I remember, in the first year of Greek at Vanderbilt University, if I'm not mistaken. And, besides, we had to read some of Xenophon's *Memorabilia*, didn't we?

ELLIOTT: Yes.

DAVIDSON: And I don't think that's to be discounted, because the present philosophy classes at Vanderbilt will never read anything Greek. There's nobody in the class that would be proficient enough to read the Greek. And so there's an enormous difference between the present generation and our generation. And as to Dr. Mims, of course, I never knew that English and American literature existed until I got into Dr. Mims's class. They just were simply phantoms for me. I didn't know they had any history, and didn't know anything about it. And he drove us into it, literally, shouted at us until we took hold, somehow. And even if you responded negatively, if you didn't like the kind of teaching he did, there was something there you had to do. You were just carried on irresistibly. I think that's rather important.

TATE: To go back to the Greek, though, I think we ought to mention the name of Herbert Tolman, who was one of the greatest scholars in this country and one of the greatest human beings I've ever known.

ELLIOTT: Well, Tolman was a very great scholar in the complete sense of the term—

TATE: Yes.

ELLIOTT: —and he could transmit this to people in a very magical way. There was a real charisma, if there's a meaning to that word—

TATE: Charisma is the right word—

ELLIOTT: —about Tolman; and there was about Alec's father, whom few of us knew except through Alec. But those who did Sanskrit—I wasn't lucky enough to do that —got this same kind of thing. Tootsie Steele* was a different order of being—

TATE: He was a great scholar in his way—

ELLIOTT: —but a very great scholar in his own way.

TATE: But not the great teacher that Tolman was.

ELLIOTT: No, nothing like the same. But he did teach you a respect for the discipline of Latin, at any rate, and some of the—

STEVENSON: Bill, could I go back to Dr. Tolman for a minute here—

ELLIOTT: I wish you would.

TATE: I do, too.

STEVENSON: —and add a word or two to that? Dr. Tolman,

* R. B. Steele, Professor of Latin.

as Bill has said, was a complete scholar and a complete gentleman—

TATE: Absolutely.

STEVENSON: —a man of great charm. And his interest in all the languages was not only that of a research man, an analyst, but also that, I think, really of a poet. He used to read the Greek aloud to us, as all of us that took it remember; and his translations of it were not only accurate but rhythmical, in a sonorous style that made the—

TATE: Very beautiful style.

ELLIOTT: He could make the word "contiguous" a poetic word [*laughter*]—

TATE: Exactly.

ELLIOTT: —in reading *Oedipus Tyrannus*.

STEVENSON: At the same time I would say he was certainly not an easy teacher. And those of us that managed to get through the third year of Greek and struggle through the tragedians and the comedians of Greek literature, and even essayed Pindar, and I do mean *essayed*—

ELLIOTT: That was about as far as it got.

STEVENSON: —found out he was not an easy taskmaster at all. But he had an enormous influence, I am quite willing to admit, on what poetry I have written. I couldn't identify it quite clearly, but it was certainly there. I'd like to pass on for just a moment to a name that perhaps some of us have forgotten only temporarily, and that was St. George L. Sioussat,* who did more for me personally in history than any man before or since, and in many respects was one of the most original minds and one of the most sarcastic minds I ever encountered. But I learned a lot more in one term of Sioussat's history than I learned in all the other years I took it.

* Professor of History.

LYTLE: He wasn't here when I was here, was he?

TATE: No, he had gone by the time you came along.

ELLIOTT: But he was certainly of that order. There were many other people: I don't think anybody could ever forget Dyer—the sociologist, what's his name?

TATE: Gus Dyer, Gus, Gus.

ELLIOTT: —because Johnny used to say that to hear Gus Dyer say, "I do love to hear a horse eat corn," in a deep bass voice was really a great experience. [*laughter*] And he at least had a certain earthiness, a realism about his approaches to sociology, which is a thing not often taught in that way.

TATE: I never took a course.

ELLIOTT: Oh, yes, but these rich, flavorful people, you know, had a very great deal to do with your understanding of things in an entirely different way from getting them at least in—

THORP: What about the teaching of Latin poetry? Nobody's said anything about that.

TATE: Well, Dr. Steele did most of that.

ELLIOTT: And Horace was not in style.

RANSOM: He was very good at Horace, I think.

TATE: Yes.

ELLIOTT: Well, you remember, there used to be jokes marked in the books, and the class would dutifully laugh at the point that the joke was marked in the book, because it was otherwise sometimes undistinguishable—

TATE: And you didn't know whether to laugh or not. At least—

ELLIOTT: —but they were marked. And on one occasion he forgot to tell one of these jokes and they laughed anyhow.

[*laughter*] He looked mildly surprised and looked around with a rather pained expression, and said, "Young gentlemen, you should emend your texts from generation to generation." [*laughter*] Now, you know that kind of quality was really one for Horace, whether art was half woman and half fish or not.

TATE: Now, Bill, was Dr. Steele's hair in two colors, or three? There was a patch of red on it, then it would be gray—mottled, it was a mottled—

ELLIOTT: I never counted them—

TATE: I think there were three.

ELLIOTT: —but there was certainly a multiform effect, a multicolor.

BROOKS: One way perhaps to point up the possible importance of some of these courses and people is to make this brief note: that for me, coming a few years later, the whole spectrum was greatly changed. Tolman was not here—

ELLIOTT: No.

BROOKS: —Tootsie Steele was so old by that time that he was a kind of glamorous name; I mean I got nothing out of the course. And so it went. It may well be that there was a very lively and fine configuration just at that time, and within five or six years the thing had changed.

WARREN: It'd changed greatly by my time.

ELLIOTT: Well, there was a practicing French poet who was here at that time. Unhappily, I can't remember his name. He had almost no teeth left. But he was quite an interesting fellow. He didn't last very long, and it's too bad, because he was a man of considerable parts; but he had odd habits. And then old Bert Young,* who was, I think, negligible in his effects on us, though he was a very sweet character. Some

* Professor of French.

of these interlopers—Who was the Russian who got so angry at Walter Clyde Curry one night at the Calumet Club for giving a straight version of Aristotle's theory of catharsis and tragedy? Do you remember that? What was that Russian's name? He taught mathematics. These were flavorful people, and Vanderbilt was rather fortunate, I think, in getting these odd bits and pieces of flotsam that had some real quality in them, you know.

THORP: Do you think, Cleanth, that it changed really markedly? Because we may be on a very, very important point here: that these professors had a considerable—

BROOKS: Well, we would certainly have to have confirmation. After all, a freshman or sophomore giving you his impressions twenty-five or thirty years later; I may be badly off. All I'm saying is that Tolman was a legend which was alive enough—I would hear wonderful stories, about what Tootsie Steele had been, and so on. But I was strangely imperceptive, or the spectrum had really changed. I wonder if anybody else in the period—

DAVIDSON: I could add something there. My recollection is, if John will confirm it, that Vanderbilt was the last university in the country to drop the requirement of Greek for the B.A. degree, and I think that was shortly after World War I.

BETHURUM: It was dropped in my junior year, and fortunately I'd already started on Greek.

DAVIDSON: Well, what year was that, Dorothy?

BETHURUM: Well, that was 1918.

DAVIDSON: Yes.

THORP: Exactly the year Hamilton College dropped it; and I dropped it in my junior year.

BETHURUM: Well, I went on and took it, and then took some more, too; because I had, by that time, become infatuated.

But I can remember the horror with which I heard it was being dropped; I heard it from Dr. Sanborn, who thought the foundations of the University had been shaken, and—

TATE: And they were.

ELLIOTT: Well, nothing is more pleasant than this reminiscing, and I think we certainly ought to say something about Walter Clyde Curry, who surely had as deep an impact on people who studied Chaucer and other things with him; he just opened up new depths of scholarship. I studied Chaucer and Shakespeare with Johnny, first, and I came back to Chaucer because I was interested in it and worked with Walter Clyde. And his ripeness of scholarship and his curious learning and quirks of mind were really quite refreshing. And the surprise element that's so essential to poetry I think he introduced us to, in characterization, and things of that sort.

TATE: I remember Curry in those days—well, of course, he was a bachelor and I think perhaps he was the last one of our teachers, you see, to get married—he was enormously hospitable to all the younger people. I remember Red and I used to practically live in his room there and—

WARREN: Borrow his typewriter.

TATE: —we'd borrow his typewriter. And he had infinite patience with us.

RANSOM: A very good talker.

TATE: Excellent talker.

ELLIOTT: Wonderful man, always with his pipe, smoke-curing our learning.

TATE: Yes.

WARREN: There's one factor, I think—I don't know how to assess it, really, but in a small and close provincial college, anybody who's there who has quality on the faculty stands out like a diamond on a piece of black velvet, you see. I mean if you had five able students of philosophy on the faculty, it would sort of cancel out, in a way. It ceases to be something; it just becomes then a convenience for you for passing a course or fulfilling the requirements. And the limitations made a kind of a personal focus on individuals and on ideas; I remember this quite distinctly, since some of these people represented the great world of ideas and the great world of geography, of wider horizons, in a very special way which is no longer true in educational institutions, I suppose. So once given, by accident, certain persons on the faculty, their impact is much greater than it would be otherwise. Now the other night I was at dinner at Northrop's house in New Haven. An eminent professor of law was there, and he and Northrop were talking about big world universities and certain small colleges. And they both had made surveys and had been around a lot, and this professor of law had actually made trips around looking at small colleges. It started by Northrop saying that when you had very large departments of philosophy, or other large departments where there were a lot of high-powered people, the students didn't learn how to think, because they didn't follow one man closely enough to see how his mind worked, for better or for worse, on a problem. They only took his view and put it down as "that's what he thinks"; they didn't follow the process, because they were never with him enough. If you had five different courses in philosophy with five different people—and all of them splendid, let us say, or not splendid, or something, but they are different—you'd never learn how one of them thought at all. You never followed his thinking.

TATE: Red, you remember—

WARREN: And they had no sense of the process of his mind— excuse me [to Tate]. Northrop was saying, well, something is lost by the accumulation of a lot of really first-rate people under one academic roof. It becomes a cafeteria of intellects, then, rather than a good square meal where you follow through the way a few people think or feel, and have a model to accept or reject.

TATE: I think there were three men like that at Vanderbilt in our time: John, Tolman, and Sanborn. And we had them right through from the beginning. We weren't shopping around.

ELLIOTT: We took all the courses that they offered—

DAVIDSON: And I'd like to add, too, that we had very easy personal access to them, at any time—

WARREN: That's right, and all the personal relations.

DAVIDSON: —this was continued with talking among ourselves constantly. From 1914 to somewhere in the early 1930's, when I look back on it, it seems to me the period of the best conversation and intimate intercourse that I've ever enjoyed in my life; and since then there's been nothing to equal it, because the college community that we had then has just disappeared; it's broken up.

WARREN: By the time I came along, you see, the faculty was larger. Don was teaching by that time, and Curry was teaching, and so there was a little more variety in that sense. But still the atmosphere was the same.

LYTLE: Red, I remember—really this was the shock of illumination, John. I mean, I had written something for you, and you told Red—it's this indirect business, not even the direct and easy access—and John had said that it was like a man playing a fiddle well on one string. [*laughter*] And Red told me that, and that was really the shock, you know, that set me on one string with it, you see. Red had a profound effect on me.

JACOBS: Gentlemen, you have mentioned, I believe, medieval studies, Shakespeare, the nineteenth century, and the classics in the light of Mr. Tate's poems about Alexander Pope, in the light of the well-known metaphysical techniques. What did you have in the seventeenth and eighteenth centuries? You discovered that on your own?

ELLIOTT: That was fresh discovery, and all the more interesting for that reason. Well, we did have some things; Johnny used to talk about Milton.

TATE: Johnny used to talk about Donne, too.

ELLIOTT: Donne, yes, a little bit; but there were no systematic courses of the normal type, where you were just dragged through by the scruff of the neck.

THORP: I'm sure there's a lot about this matter in Louise Cowan's work, but something I'd like to bring up here: in the sessions, the actual meetings of the Fugitives, what was the type of the criticism? Was it any attempt to bring people along to a party line? Was it anything that you could call a center to the discussion, a center to the criticism?

TATE: Well, Willard, I would just say that we'd read the poems, and somebody would say, "That's a very bad line, you've got to change that. This word won't do." I mean it was minute and practical to a great extent. Of course, there were general discussions of poetry, but I think it was mostly focused on this practical thing, as I recall it.

WARREN: One thing that strikes me in recollection, now: a few years after I left Vanderbilt, and people began to refer to those people as a unit, you see, as if there were a church or an orthodoxy; and I was so shocked by that—

TATE: I was, too; I had no idea—

WARREN: —because I was so aware of the differences of temperament, and the differences of opinions, you see, in conversation—the Fugitive meetings were outside—but the notion of a unity had just never occurred to me, really, except that the unity was just purely a unity of friendship and common background.

TATE: It was always a—I'm sure John is tired of these compliments we are paying him, but I want to pay him one more: that you think of other people who turned out poets, you see, in the way that, say, Yvor Winters—Yvor Winters insists that all his students are to become exact duplicates of himself. John not only didn't insist on that, he didn't want it.

RANSOM: I think we might mention for the record that we finally developed a standard procedure: no one could come and read a poem without a supply of carbons to pass around among all present. And, therefore, it was based on the study of the written word—that is, the critical remark. And it passed around to everybody. And that went on for the four years, possibly a year before we began to publish, and then for the four years in which we published *The Fugitive* magazine. Now by the end of that time I should think that a very obvious, but possibly not the universal kind of conclusion, was reached; it was more or less unconscious but very statesmanlike. *The Fugitive* magazine was solvent; we had no debts. And by that time we knew each other's personalities so thoroughly that we could anticipate the response that would be made by anyone in the group to the poem under discussion. And, therefore, we had drained each other dry. What should have happened, though it was not in the cards, was to separate for four years and then to return to the same thing again. Instead of that, we turned to something else. But we had the good sense—before there was an ill-will, before we had begun to fuss very much, and while we were still solvent—we closed out *The Fugitive* magazine.

ELLIOTT: Of course, I wasn't here for two or three of the most critical years; I came back from Oxford to spend the summer here only. So I can't speak with anything like the experience that you fellows had who were present throughout the whole period. But in the beginnings and in those interim periods when I was sampling what I thought was the Fugitive technique, I thought I discerned a very interesting development of something very like a party line for most of the group. There was a hardening of taste, if I may put it that way, that insisted upon a certain novelty of treatment in poetry that was perceptibly a little bit irritated at just rhyme and just meter. They still accepted this, and everybody wrote things of that sort, but they were playing with disguised effects; and Johnny introduced us to the false rhyme, and to many effects of that sort, and we began studying techniques of poetry, by experiment and indirection and then comparison of models—quoting models—so that there was a fairly, if I can say so, uniform standard of aesthetic criticism about what was a good poetic line. And this, I think, would be borne out. When I wrote poems like "Black Man," for instance, and in an entirely different meter and manner, they had a certain shock on the group. And yet I was influenced in some parts of that poem, I am sure, by the feeling that my peers would not like some things if I did them that way. I still went ahead and did some of them pretty much that way.

TATE: Well, Bill, I think John was the only one of us who experimented with the slant rhymes, or off-rhymes.

ELLIOTT: Oh, no, I think you'd find that this was repeated by other people, and not less successfully.

TATE: Not much, Bill. What poem?

STEVENSON: "Meuse Heights."

ELLIOTT: Well, sure.

STEVENSON: It's the only one I can think of offhand.

TATE: Yes.

ELLIOTT: Yes, that's right. And there were people who did it. I think that Don held out probably more valiantly than anybody for his own ear. And I was on that side, if anybody; I thought that we underrated musical effects; they were thought to be "too easy" by most members of the group. I know this was Allen's tightly-seeded lyric. The—

TATE: Well, I've changed my mind about all that.

ELLIOTT: Well, that's good, that's good. [*laughter*]

STARR: I think something ought to be said about the decision to remain anonymous in the early *Fugitives,* and then the decision to give up anonymity. That might be helpful for the record.

TATE: Why did we have the pseudonyms? I've forgotten.

RANSOM: We had just adopted a name, *The Fugitive.* No one was quite sure why. It seemed to be a secret among us, though no one knew what the secret was. And it was just— then a certain awe at the thought that we were breaking into print. We were simply founding a magazine to print our own stuff, and that seemed a very bold thing to do. And so we thought that we would conserve a certain sense of mystery by hiding our authorship, and therefore we invented names that were probably quite significant—

TATE: I think they were, too.

RANSOM: —for the first number or two. Was it one number or more than one number? It was more than one number.

TATE: Was it two?

COWAN: (*at the same time*) It was two. Two.

WARREN: Merrill, what was your name? I forget.

TATE: What?

WARREN: What was Merrill's? Is Merrill here?

TATE: "Dendric"; Merrill was "Dendric" [*Cowan and others repeat the name simultaneously*]

WARREN: "Dendric," that's right.

TATE: Very appropriate.

WARREN: Some of the names were certainly some of the happiest poetic strokes of the author. [*laughter*]

TATE: "Robin Gallivant." *

COWAN: "Robin Gallivant."

TATE: "Roger Prim" ** [*laughter*]

STEVENSON: "Drimlonigher" ***

ELLIOTT: How do you pronounce that, Alec?

STEVENSON: "Drim-lon-e-gar."

THORP: Did you invent your own, or were they given by the group?

ELLIOTT: [*amidst others*] No, we invented our own.

BEATTY: Weren't you "Feathertop," Allen?

TATE: "Feathertop."

RANSOM: "Henry Feathertop." [*laughter*] Hawthorne.

RUBIN: Who thought up the name *Fugitive?*

TATE: Sidney Hirsch, as I remember it.

ELLIOTT: Yes, I think it was Sidney's—

RANSOM: Sidney, I think.

ELLIOTT: This was a basic contribution; as I said last night, I think it set the esoteric tone.

RANSOM: Didn't you have it that way, Mrs. Cowan?

COWAN: Well, there was some disagreement about that.

TATE: Oh, I think Sidney did it.

ELLIOTT: Oh, I don't think there's much question that Sidney's esoteric and highly mystical and escapist ideas— he cloaked himself in mystagogy that really made him very important. Merrill wrote a very interesting poem about that. Where is Merrill?

* Donald Davidson.
** John Crowe Ransom.
*** Alec B. Stevenson.

WILLS: Merrill is not here.

RUBIN: Merrill had to wait for a long distance call; he's coming this evening.

ELLIOTT: Well, at any rate, it's the poem about the owl's wings and so on, the magician. And Sidney had this dominating, almost mesmeric—

WILLS: There's Merrill now.

ELLIOTT: —habit of addressing people in the Socratic manner. He had lain on his back—whether he had a psychic or other back injury—he had something of that kind. He had given up writing plays, even the Greek Pageants, performed with such éclat at our Parthenon. He had written successful plays in New York—or more or less successful ones—like *The Passion Play of Washington Square;* he had lived everywhere in the world. He had lived in China, you know; he'd lived in Paris as a model; he'd lived in New York. And here was a man of really rare qualities: he was no Miniver Cheevy, or anything of that sort, or any of the other characters of Edwin Arlington Robinson—he was a combination of the tremendously robust and powerful figure, with in some ways this twist of mystagogy. I'd pay this tribute to Sidney: the insights that he had about the struggle of myths and systems, and the nature of the struggle of the people who became the epic exemplars, was superior in its political insight to any figure I've known, in its anticipation of this shape of things to come. For whatever reasons he did it, Sidney wrote a poem which was characteristic of his philosophy, about "The Fugitive Blacksmith," and he was always talking of this "stranger," the Athenian stranger. He studied Plato very deeply and we wrangled about Plato all the time; this was a regular kick-off on all our earlier evenings at his house and at Mr. Frank's. And this Fugitive Blacksmith, I think, was his trademark; if he didn't do anything else, he was determined to put this stamp on us, to recognize the esoteric mysteries of *his* system. Then the group rather weak-mindedly accepted the name *Fugitive,* I think, just out of a sense of concession: we were all meeting at Mr. Frank's house, where Sidney lived, supported like a true mystic. Mr. Jim Frank ought to be mentioned as one of the great sweet persons of all we knew, who gave us— this old Scots fellow, who was Jewish and Scotch, a metaphysician in—

RANSOM: A Thirty-Third Degree Mason.

ELLIOTT: Yes, that's right. A very deep mind, but very, very quiet and reserved and—

TATE: You know he wrote a few short poems—

ELLIOTT: That's right.

TATE: —a few only, but they were very graceful and I always remembered the diction was pure.

ELLIOTT: Pure, that's the right word for him, and for his poems. And I think out of gratitude for that, as much as anything else, we sort of accepted this name. Would that check with you, Johnny, and Don?

DAVIDSON: I think you are right in general principle, but my recollection is, and I'll ask Steve to confirm it, that Alec Stevenson suggested our use of the actual name itself, though it should come from the source.

ELLIOTT: Well, how did you hit it?

STEVENSON: Well, I think the background is precisely as you've described it, Bill, and we were talking about a name for the magazine, and we had had so much conversation and so many discussions with Sidney over a long period of time that I think more or less by accident I said, "Well, why don't we call it *The Fugitive?*" It was as simple and as unintellectual as that.

ELLIOTT: It was partly in gratitude for the hospitality and Sidney's dialectical leadership?

STEVENSON: Yes.

ELLIOTT: That is, because we had met at this house, and Sidney had been the true begetter in a sense, because in these discussions he had such a dominant character. You had almost to break away from Sidney, eventually, at some state—and we all did, I suppose, in one way or another—in order to just get clear of this hypnotic, mesmeric kind of an influence. But there's no question at all about the power of his mind; and it's very sad that he has absented himself from this performance. It isn't a Fugitive meeting without him.

STARR: Let me say a word about him. What Elliott has just said is certainly true, that everybody had to break with him —intellectually break with him—because there were curious quirks in his dogma, which it was, dogma. His was a remarkable mind; you might say an untrained mind: he was anti-logic. If we'd proceed, as we all do, from a postulate to a conclusion by a certain path through our brain, let us say, he regarded that as not being really valid. He would prefer to jump from this point to that point. It was a kind of really unorthodox thinking. I've lived here in Nashville all my life, and yet I haven't seen him for thirty years— there was no overt break, but just a drifting apart—nor have I spoken to him. But as I recall his own philosophy, it was something like this: that he believed in the wisdom of the Ancients; he believed that there was nothing new, and that all of the good things, all of the truths in this world, were essentially esoteric; and that the people handed down these truths as the really great heritage from one generation to another, always carefully concealed. I didn't understand that part, nor do I now: as to why they had to be concealed. But the truths were available only to the superior people who were capable of seeing them; and they had to be handed down in the form of myths. Now it would not surprise me to learn—and, of course, I can only guess— that *The Fugitive,* or a publication, was very much desired by Sidney Hirsch, in order—in some mystical way—for him to communicate with people; I mean actually communicate with living people somewhere.

TATE: They are the initiates, throughout the world.

STARR: With the initiates, yes—

ELLIOTT: Even with this conviction that there were initiates who understood this, and that they communicated with him in ways only understood by the few initiates—

STARR: Yes, and that afterward, perhaps, his feeling was that "I am not terribly interested in poetry as poetry." That's just a footnote.

RANSOM: I think he was the man who proposed publication first.

TATE: Yes he did. I'm sure of that.

STARR: Yes, he was.

DAVIDSON: Then he also had the idea, Alfred, that if you were a true poet, you knew this secret lore intuitively. You remember he expounded on that; and, therefore, if Bill Elliott would write a poem, or John would write one, containing one of the words from which esoteric symbolism might be deduced, he would immediately in the criticism fall on that word and begin to expound; and he might then lead you right to the passage in the *Odyssey* where Polyphemus asks Odysseus his name and he tells him—what was it?; Outis or was it Metis?

STARR: He was certainly the most curious—

DAVIDSON: And then he would go from that point to Shakespeare or to Dante or various other writers, who he claimed all possessed this secret lore, and it all linked together.

TATE: But the curious thing about him, he would never take the trouble to learn any of these languages. And his derivations were always just wild, you know. The Trojan horse was the mad horse because the Middle English word for mad is *wod;* and by the time he would say something like that, you would be so dizzy you didn't think about it. [*laughter*]

ELLIOTT: And developed on over to the wolf, the *Feltro,* in Dante, and so on. But all this was the "fugitive," you see, because you had to escape detection and you had to operate in a subterranean and a covert activity. Sidney's the greatest covert actor of our times. I've often thought that if he could ever be harnessed, he would make a wonderful fellow to put on some things now, but you couldn't harness him. The one harness that he ever submitted to was the dictionary. He had this enormous dictionary, in the largest size, and he would take you to it and thumb through it and he would find the most remarkable derivations, and some of them were extraordinarily interesting. They were not all wild, though they were not philologically disciplined. That there was an esoteric tradition in Plato, no one can doubt. The numerology of Plato, for instance, which Jowett is pleased to say he is throwing dust in our eyes—albeit "stardust"—is there; and the "achromatic" philosophy of Aristotle, which Alexander reproaches his ex-tutor for revealing, you see, the secret doctrines of which he was too careless with, and so on. And, of course, we got glimpses of the cabala and all sorts of things, picked up in this odd, miscellaneous, and completely undisciplined way. But that he taught us some interesting words and their relationship to symbols and to mystic doctrines and their poetic significance in that sense, I think there is no question at all.

DAVIDSON: One of those, I might add: you remember that he would take the parable of the sower, thirtyfold, sixtyfold, a hundredfold, then jump right over to Tennyson's *Idylls of the King,* and have Gareth conquering all those knights thirtyfold, sixtyfold, a hundredfold, you remember—thirty knights, sixty knights, a hundred knights, in three separate adventures; then go on from that point to discover thirty, sixty, a hundred, all around, everywhere.

ELLIOTT: Yes, in the proportions of the Parthenon, everything, you see. And this was all according to numerology and Pythagorean and Masonic doctrines: the Greeks got it from the Egyptians, and the Egyptians from heaven knows whom; he was privy to this, but he didn't reveal it. He should be here. You must feel his power to understand his part in our beginnings.

BROOKS: I think I've had a signal from our host—though this is an ungracious thing to break this wonderful tide of talk—that there are some refreshments awaiting us, and maybe this is a good time to stop.

WILLS: We don't want to break it up, when, after all, you must talk about Sidney a long time and then nobody— [*laughter and general conversation*]

ELLIOTT: An endless topic.

THIRD SESSION

Friday Afternoon, May 4

Moderator: JOHN CROWE RANSOM

BROOKS: I think it's time, perhaps, for us to begin. It's a little after two. I express the happiness of all of us at seeing Mr. Hirsch here with us. And Mr. Ransom has kindly said that he would act as moderator, or general steerer for this session. So I am without further ado going to turn the meeting over to John.

RANSOM: I didn't make the suggestion originally, I want you to know. I am—

BROOKS: He was dragged quite reluctantly.

RANSOM: —happy to serve in this manner. And I want first of all to welcome Sidney Hirsch; our meetings haven't felt right without him, and we were not complete. He could have heard his name many times this morning; we were discussing the contribution of various of the original members, and his primary part in founding the magazine and in assuring us about the name, and the way he elevated the discussion and the theme at all times. I won't call for a speech from him, but I do hope that he will speak to the various questions that come up. Now as to the questions that we should take up next, I'd be very glad to have a good suggestion; it might be much better than the one I have in mind. I had thought that possibly we could get into some

of the characteristic Fugitive prejudice—dogma it might be
—about what makes good poetry, if we just called for a little
talk about what's the matter with poetry today, or what's
good and what's deficient in it? Not many Fugitives are still
producing poetry, but I think we are very objective in looking at modern poetry. And I would like for Mr. Tate to
lead off by talking about the poetic scene at this moment,
and some very pointed talk about young poets and about
poems in general as they go in this age.

TATE: Well, John, I think we talked a little about that
yesterday evening. It seems to me that we've got, since our
time, perhaps two new literary generations which, in this
country at any rate, follow upon one another very rapidly;
and I think they've developed what might be called a period
style. I would think that this is not a matter of statistics, but
simply a kind of figure of speech: whereas today perhaps we
have twenty very gifted young poets—who write this anonymous period style—back in the early twenties it was impossible. Poets were much more original, or they couldn't write
at all. The literary tradition in the United States, and particularly in the South at the end of the First World War,
was not usable; that is, we couldn't take off from our elders:
there was nothing there. And I would think that the poetic
revolution of this century has about run its course; and it
has developed into a period style in which there's nothing
new to be expected. I don't like to call names, but the names
will be obvious to you, too. I have the feeling in reading
through some of their books that they are highly accomplished, but you can't tell one poem from another, and often
you can't tell one poet from another when they appear in
the best literary magazines today. On the other hand, I
suppose if a new school of poetry started today, we would
be the last people to recognize it; we are so confirmed in
our literary habits; and I don't suppose it would be up to
us to recognize it. I don't know what else to speak on this
topic, John; I feel very little interest in the literary scene.

RANSOM: There's very little interest in the literary scene; you are a patriarch, and—

TATE: Well, not yet. [*laughter*]

RUBIN: Allen, how much of that do you think you all have done?

TATE: Well, I wouldn't know in the case of any one of us, but I do think that there has been, say, a stretch of time between John Ransom and Robert Lowell, when a great deal happened; and the younger poets don't show as much versatility and resourcefulness as their elders did in their time. I wouldn't know who had been influenced by whom. Oh, in some cases you can see traces of specific influence which—

RANSOM: Well, then, there's an associated question that was started last night, but it didn't go far: Why did the Fugitives stop writing poetry?

TATE: Well, have they?

RANSOM: I know Merrill has not stopped—

TATE: Have they, really? Don wrote two new ones this winter.

RANSOM: There are several—

HIRSCH: Haven't you written a fine long poem, Allen?

TATE: Well, I've written a long poem, yes.

HIRSCH: It appeared in *The Partisan Review* in the first part?

TATE: Yes, and the others are on the way, but—

HIRSCH: I thought that was a great poem.

TATE: Well, thank you, Sidney.

RANSOM: Would you talk a little bit to that? Now, you haven't talked your share, Mr. Hirsch. What makes a great poem? What made that poem—?

HIRSCH: Well, this is something that we used to discuss at

great length. I think that the subject matter is very important. Now, I think Mr. Tate has a very great poem in that—What is the name of it?

TATE: "The Maimed Man."

HIRSCH: "The Maimed Man." A very great poem. I suppose everyone here is familiar with it. This takes us back, it takes me back, to many discussions we had.

MOORE: I'd like to hear more about Allen's poem, and your critique of it, Sidney.

HIRSCH: Well, I think it's a great poem, a great poem. I think Tate is a great poet. I told him so twenty-five years ago; I don't believe he believed me.

RANSOM: Well, Allen, couldn't you recite—

TATE: [at the same time] Well, Sidney, I still can't believe you, but I like what you say very much. [laughter]

RANSOM: Don't you remember that poem? Couldn't you recite—

TATE: Don will use my failure of memory here to point up his thesis; so I can't remember.

TATE: Merrill wanted us to have an old time meeting. Well, I said that would rule me out: bring a new poem. Merrill would give the program pretty well.

RUBIN: Allen, what are some of—I don't know if this is a fair question—but do you see any difference in your problem in writing that poem and in the problems you had writing poems during the days of *The Fugitive*? And what are they, if you do?

TATE: Well, I don't like to use the word *problems* about poetry.

RUBIN: I didn't mean the problem of the poem, but the problem of the poet.

TATE: I don't see the problem of the poet apart from the problem of each specific poem.

RUBIN: Well, you've got me there.

TATE: I don't think the poet exists except when he's writing the poem; otherwise he's just a human being.

RUBIN: I stand contradicted.

TATE: Yes. Don't you feel that way?

MOORE: Yes, I think so.

ELLIOTT: Isn't there something nevertheless in the state of being of *a* particular poet which remains through a succession of poems?

TATE: Oh, yes, that's quite true.

ELLIOTT: And therefore I think that the poet is a poet perhaps apart from the act of a poem, *a* poem. He is a poet in terms of the poems that he puts together.

TATE: Well, if he intends to wait around until he can write the next one, it may be some years before that happens, and he has to fill up his time between poems.

ELLIOTT: That really isn't quite adequate to my point. I dare say, Allen, with all your development you are still very much Allen Tate as a poet, and that you'd be recognizable; but the criticism that you make of the younger poets would certainly never apply to you. I think this same thing would be true of Penn Warren—unmistakably of Penn Warren in his other writings, and I dare say almost equal in his poems: that there is a something that stamps the artist as an artist, and the question is whether you can compare them and whether the subject matter that they treat has any bearing on the superiority, or the lack of it, of the product. And I think it's very interesting to look at Red's novels and his poems and try to trace through them some sort of a pattern of the spirit.

TATE: There's a continuity.

ELLIOTT: There is a continuity. And the topics that he deals with are extremely interesting from the point of view of the revelation of the focus of drama and tragedy that he's trying to develop; therefore, the subject matter does have some basic bearing on the topic.

RANSOM: Well, I think there's a metaphorical quality to Warren's prose—which means a poetic quality—that's quite sharp; at the same time, there's sometimes a rhetorical quality to the poetry which is verified, and that's a prose virtue that has come in there. I don't think that he's as pure, and therefore—I know he has written about "impure" poetry in preference to "pure," but I don't think that he has been a poet entirely like the rest of us: he's been bolder in the sense that there's a nicer mixture of prose virtues and poetic virtues, I think, in his poetry.

MOORE: Could I say a word, John? I know this is an understatement, but I would say that of all of us you and your style are the most complicated. I've read all of your poems repeatedly; I know many of them by heart. In them I find the richness of a fruit cake, let us say, as compared with ordinary cake. I think that Allen's style is what I would call the most elegant; and by elegant I mean as a highly refined and very, very, precisely written and expressed medium. Red's poems and novels to me are the most dramatic. I see just what you've pointed out; I've thought of it, and I'm glad you mentioned it: this reflection of his poetry on his prose, and reflection of his prose in his poetry. He has achieved a kind of synthesis, or fusion, or fission or something there, that no one else of us has done. I would say that he is certainly the most dramatic. For example, his latest novel. I can easily see it written as a poem; and we do know that he did write *All the King's Men* as a poem first. Isn't that right, Red?

WARREN: That's right. It was a verse play.

MOORE: And then I've been trying to think where I come in this picture. I would say that I am the most documentary; that I take little minutes and make little moments, or monuments, out of them; and that's all I do and all I've ever done. But now I'd like to drag the conversation back to where we were last night, if we could, and get Sidney Hirsch to comment again on the point we started and didn't get very far on. We started out, and immediately the subject —as I recall, it was pointed out that *The Fugitive* was full of little short poems. And we stopped, going off into other fields. Then the question arose, why didn't we write longer poems, or why had no one written, let us say, anything comparable to an epic? I remember what Alfred Starr said last night about that; and I wondered if he would repeat, in capsule, or if Tate would repeat, what was said last night? I think that's the main argument that we are on, and we ought to stick to it until we get somewhere.

RANSOM: I think that that is a fine topic to introduce, especially for the sake of hearing Sidney Hirsch on it. I hope we won't be repetitive any more than we can help in going over that ground. But I would very much welcome—

TATE: John, won't you restate the topic, then, so Sidney will—?

RANSOM: Well, the topic was raised by Bill Elliott, in the first place: why the Fugitives wrote no epic poems. And there were various responses, and the discussion veered in various ways. And then Alfred Starr's point was, I think, that he wasn't concerned so much with the idea of epic, or the definition of epic, but the thought that the Fugitives may not have squarely faced reality; and it might have been ivory-tower poetry. He didn't use those terms; I don't recall the precise words, but I think that was the gist of it. And so we were more or less stalled at that point. I think I made the point—but it was not well received—that I thought that the poet William Butler Yeats had a lesson for us there; that he matured into a period when his whole mind was active in his poetry; and he frankly went into politics with poetry —though he never debased poetry; he coarsened it, but I think not debased it—in his attempt to get into public affairs with poetry and have the poet count. Now it might be that Sidney Hirsch doesn't want the poet to have that kind of a role, that that might be vulgarizing. I'd like to know what he might think of that.

HIRSCH: Well, John Ransom, that is, of course, a matter of great interest to me, of great importance; and I've given it some considerable thought. I've thought especially about two poems that appeared in *The Fugitive*, one of yours— I believe it was called "Two Gentlemen in Bonds," wasn't i? One about the *logos endiathetos*, and one about *logos prophorikos*. Am I correct? Pardon?

RANSOM: I think so. That was a sonnet sequence.

HIRSCH: Sonnet sequence—and Mr. Tate's poem, "The Cross." Do you remember that? You gave me the manuscript of that. Those two poems interested me, of course, greatly, because of a statement by Plato: you recall Plato said that the poet by genius, by flashes of genius, often penetrates into the heart of the mysteries, often understands what the philosopher learns by his studies? Do you recall that? Now, I discussed that poem, "The Cross," with Mr. Tate at the time; as I say, he gave me the manuscript. I'd like to ask you now, does he remember it very well? Do you recall all that you had in it?

TATE: I think I remember pretty well, yes.

HIRSCH: When we discussed it, you said, "I was unaware at the time of writing it that I had these elements in it."

TATE: Yes, that's true.

HIRSCH: Are you aware of them now? May I ask—

TATE: I'm much more aware of them than I was then, yes.

HIRSCH: It's a very amazing thing that he uses certain Platonic terms and certain Greek words—gives the derivations and has paronomasia on them—which he informed me at the time that he did not know, was not aware of. Am I correct about that?

TATE: Yes.

HIRSCH: You are now?

TATE: Yes, much more so.

HIRSCH: Well, don't you think that's very interesting? Don't you think that poem was approaching epic quality? Does everyone here remember the poem?

RANSOM: Yes.

HIRSCH: Again, I say I think it was a very great poem. Then in Mr. Ransom's poem on "Jesus and Paul"—am I correct there?

RANSOM: That had another title: "Our Two Worthies."

HIRSCH: Yes, "Our Two Worthies." And, again, Plato uses those two terms and he calls them, as you recall, *logos endiathetos* and *logos prophorikos*. Now I'd like to ask if you were aware at the time that you were doing it, or did you come in the category of Plato who said that the poet arrives at these conclusions by great flashes of genius? Is it a fair question to ask?

RANSOM: Yes, it is. Yes, I remember you said that, and that I had a feeling that my poem was more serious than it sounded. I read it not long ago and called it a nonsense poem; that is, there's a bit of automatic writing in it. But it has always seemed to me a little more serious than the intention that people generally attributed to it. I don't believe I ever went to the bottom of that, or tried to much. But I do remember your feeling about it; I was very grateful.

HIRSCH: Do you feel that I was incorrect about it? Do you really feel it was a nonsense poem?

RANSOM: No, I don't think it was.

HIRSCH: Do you think so, Bill?

ELLIOTT: No, I'm not sure that I recall this poem—

RANSOM: [at the same time] You probably don't remember it.

ELLIOTT: —clearly enough. It wasn't the one about the paraclete and the exegete, was it?

RANSOM: Yes.

ELLIOTT: Oh, I do recall that one, and I certainly wouldn't call that a nonsense poem. And Sidney would no doubt find that of some significance because he spoke of babbling as the language of the mystic, and so on, and that this was an appropriate, spontaneous production from the point of view of the insight that I suppose he's been talking about. So he might say that what appeared, then, on the surface to be nonsense might often conceal very important insights.

HIRSCH: I never noticed, though, any nonsense or any babbling in it; it seemed to be intellectualized.

RANSOM: It's a little bit rapid, and the rhymes proceed very obviously from one word to the next one; and it looks like a hurried composition. I just let it write itself in a way, in so far as it's permitted to me to do that sort of thing. Very much less studied than I usually—

ELLIOTT: I think it's a very interesting point that ought to be specially noted, because there is a Fugitive group tradition against that kind of poetry, on the general grounds that it's too facile; whereas my feeling's always been that that's sometimes the very best poetry, that it comes off pat, and that if it has any finality—and sometimes those things do have finality—they do illustrate this insight that Sidney's talking about. Now this is possibly why you felt, Johnny, that, not being a studied poem, it was not a serious poem.

RANSOM: I know that Sidney told me that Brother Craig would like that poem—he was a Methodist preacher, a great friend of my father, who was a Methodist preacher—and Brother Craig didn't like that poem. [*laughter*]

ELLIOTT: But that's not the necessary test of it.

HIRSCH: He was a very—He was a priest of God, the old gentleman, a very fine old gentleman, a very pure, high-spirited mind.

BETHURUM: Did it sound flippant to him?

HIRSCH: No, it wasn't flippant at all. We had talked a great deal—Brother Craig and I. He was an elderly gentleman, approaching eighty, and had been a man of God all his life. It was very interesting: his brothers had told me that he determined to be a priest, a minister, when he was nine years of age. And he studied that poem very carefully and talked to many preachers about it. We had many discussions; theologians used to gather at his home. And you sent him a book, your book on *God Without Thunder;* and I wrote in it: "To Brother Craig, man of God"; and he was very proud of that, and he showed it to everybody and—

RANSOM: It wasn't so much the poem, I think, but the book —now that you remind me—that, I have the impression, he didn't like; that he felt that I had fallen away—

HIRSCH: Yes, he did.

RANSOM: —and expressed himself that way, perhaps, to my father; I don't know, to someone—

HIRSCH: He had many clippings on it, though. He had a clipping from an English paper in which they said you were one of the six greatest writers in English in the world.

WARREN: Even though fallen away. [*laughter*]

HIRSCH: And I gave him the paper. The English *Manchester Guardian* wrote that, if I remember.

ELLIOTT: Well, you can't tell quite, you know, what reactions *Poems About God* will produce. My great-aunt—who lived to be a hundred and was very fond of Johnny, and always traced our genealogies to include him in—was not a woman of God. She was, in fact, one of the supreme agnostics that I've ever known, and generally took the view that mankind was too little to know anything about God. And she summarized Johnny's book by saying, "Willie, what does Johnny Ransom know about God?" [*laughter*] I said, "That would be the point: that he didn't know."

HIRSCH: I think this is a matter of great importance, because it's where the Fugitives were somewhat divided. Some of us felt that subject matter—lofty subject matter—was of the greatest importance, and demonstrated whether the poem was great or not. I think some of the others believed that the treatment, the stylization, prosody, was of greater importance.

WARREN: May I speak to that point for a moment?

RANSOM: Go ahead.

WARREN: This is not said in a controversial spirit. I'm really cutting back. This last remark of Sidney's refers to something last night and again early this afternoon. I mean, it seems to me greatness is not a criterion—a profitable criterion—of poetry; that what you are concerned with is a sense of a contact with reality. And it's maybe a pinpoint touch or a whole palm of a hand laid, or something; but the important thing is the shock of this contact: a lot of current can come through a small wire. And there you are up against, well, big subjects and little subjects. It's just so it's a real subject, and, of course, you've got this word to deal with; you've got to have something that will actually create human heat in that contact. Well, language can in certain ways, because language drags the bottom of somebody into being, in one way or another, directly or indirectly. But if I had to say what I would try to hunt for in a poem— would hunt for in a poem, or would expect from a poem that I would call a poem—it would be some kind of a vital image, a vital and evaluating image, of vitality. That's a different thing from the vitality you observe or experience. It's an image of it, but it has the vital quality—it's a reflection of that vital quality, rather than a passing reflection, but it has its own kind of assurance, own kind of life, by the way it's built. And when you get around to talking about the scale, it's not the most important topic. It is an important topic, but it's something that comes in very late in the game. Now, I think we started last night with that, and it's really not our province to discuss that, except in the realm of theory—late in the game. That is, I see no difference in the degree of reality between, say, "Janet Waking" and "The Dynasts." One's a little poem, a short poem, and one's a big side-of-beef of a poem; but the significance of one can be as great as that of the other in the sense of your contact; the stab, the flash, the—I'm not arguing for short poems, now, mind you; I'm not doing a Poe thing about that, and the scale may be necessary in certain things to get the sense of reality. But there's no virtue or defect in the size one way or the other. The question is: Where do you get that image, that speaking image, the walking statue, and how would we interpret that? I would interpret it myself, but it would bring on of course a lot of wrangling and hassling about individual poems and a lot of other things. I'm not interested in getting anything said here except that—But when this problem of scale comes in early, I always begin to lose my bearings; I have to go back and start over again and try to see what it's about for myself—I don't mean writing, but I mean reading. It's that stab of some kind, early; that's the important thing for me in the sense of an image that makes that thing available to you indefinitely, so you can go back to it, can always find that peephole on the other world, you

THIRD SESSION 143

see—that moment of contact with the—well, with reality, or realness, or something.

MOORE: Could I say a word apropos of what you are talking about? Now perhaps I am speaking out of turn, and I don't mean to be too personal, but I think that—if you'll allow me to associate freely a minute—I'd like to say this: of all the Fugitive poets that have interested me most, the poems of John Ransom come first. I still can read him with the same pleasure that I read him with originally. I cannot say that of T. S. Eliot: I can no longer get much pleasure or satisfaction out of reading Mr. Eliot's poetry. But that has led me to a very careful study of Ransom's poems, and I hope some day to write an article about it. But I'll submit it to you first. Now in your first book, *Poems About God*, there are a great many revealing flashes of the kind Robert Penn Warren mentions, and I think you would say so, too, Allen. And I am sure that between your first book and the second book, the one referred to by Sidney—well, *Chills and Fever* and *Two Gentlemen in Bonds*—you have undergone as much a change in your style and your orientation as T. S. Eliot went through between his Harvard period and his early poems printed in the *Advocate* and his later poems where you see that particular Eliot style, that unmistakable trademark, emerge. Now forgive me if I am talking out of turn, but I feel that your *Poems About God* are very interesting psychologically because they are preoccupied with a debate or struggle with an identification with and against early Christian theology. I think of two particular images that are just like illuminations by a photoflash bulb: the mother baking the pie in the kitchen, I believe, and God peeping in approvingly through a door, watching —which is a very familiar image in early thinking of individuals—and I think of "The Swimmer" where you say, "Come to the top, you wicked swimmer," the man who submerges and doesn't come up. Incidentally, that is also related to your "crocodile" poem, who submerges until finally just the little nostrils of his snout stick out. Now, I didn't know what that meant, and I didn't know what a lot of the things I was writing meant—this is apropos of Sidney Hirsch's comment on Allen's poem, "The Cross," which I remember impressed me deeply, too, at the time, as a fresh, vivid, almost a religious experience—until I got to Boston, and in 1931 started an analysis with Hanns Sachs. Now, I worked with him an hour a day, five days a week, for three years; and in the course of that a great deal of my poems came up, and I had the benefit of the fact that Sachs took me as what's called a "control-analysis," or analysand, and he'd spend the summer with Freud and discuss the materials. And he brought back this interesting interpretation to me which may not be applicable to other people, but I offer it for what it's worth: that in all of our Fugitive experience, we were largely concerned with being Fugitives— whether it was a state of being or not—and at the same time being creative. But you, John, if it's not too simple an interpretation, were extracting yourself from what Don called the "cultural matrix," or the marsupial pouch of the family in home culture, and rebelling and striking off for yourself into your own style which you hit in "The Equilibrists" and "Antique Harvesters" and other poems. I found, much to my astonishment, that I was doing very much the same thing. We were all rebelling, not only against the bourbon brahmins, or the moonlight and roses, or you might call it the "moonlight and roses neurosis," or as Allen called it, the—I remember, Allen, you telling me that we were really protesting against the "sweetness and light" school; and you were right; we were.

WARREN: That was a local reference.

MOORE: That's right, a local reference. But I noticed that when my father died in 1929, I felt very depressed. And when I analyzed my depression, I found that it was because I had often fantasied he would die, or wished he would die; and when he did die, then I felt unconsciously or partly responsible. And I can say that this word *Fugitive* is absolutely our trademark. It was the proper imprint, or copyright, or whatever you want to call it, for me, and I suspect for you, John; and I think, Allen, it was to some extent for you and Red too. And, oddly enough, I had the feeling—maybe I'm wrong—that Don was, in his own way, a kind of midwife—often maternal in his kindness to us—and Sidney, I think you were a kind of gentle, non-demanding father-figure that encouraged us to rebel, to write in our own fashion, and to carry on in these Fugitive symbols and metaphors that we later diverged even further from in independent patterns of writing. Now is that just a lot of jargon, or does it make any sense, Brother Elliott? Maybe you could tell us. You are a good soul doctor.

ELLIOTT: Well, I've always been very much interested in efforts to connect poetry with conflicts in the psyche, whether they are analyzed by the school of Freud or any one of the competing schools.

MOORE: The school of hard knocks will do a good job, too.

ELLIOTT: Yes. And I think it's significant that Robert Graves —who became a Fugitive *in absentia* to some degree during this period, when he and Johnny were exchanging courtesies of bringing out each other's books, and so on—refused to let Rivers psychoanalyze him because he was afraid the wellstream of his poetry would dry up. It dried up, anyhow; it took a different form, and, of course, in time—

MOORE: Freud says—

ELLIOTT: The point that I think you are making about rebellion is universal. I mean, this is part human, and it is the mark, not only of the break between generations, the break with authority and the growing-up period of any human being, which I think is perfectly reasonable and acceptable. But the Fugitive character that I think marked this group was a somewhat split thing and between two types of Fugitives. One of them was trying to find itself in the way you've described. The other one was trying to find something that a Fugitive could flee to, or create, in a much deeper, metaphysical sense, perhaps, and was never quite satisfied with the formulations that it was making, or found, and so on. We split on that rock last night, and I don't intend to shipwreck the group again. It draws me back to this question of the subject matter of poetry in connection with this analysis. What was the subject matter that we hit upon? It was poetry of rebellion in some sense, but the form that it took—the peculiar expressions, the images, the symbols that the poets found—had a connection with that vitality that Red was talking about. And the other words that he used—I note these words with great interest when he admitted that everything was wrapped up in them and had to be unwrapped to find out what it meant—*reality* and *realness*. The image was to have, if I remember, a vital relationship to the vitality, to a vitality which was to be reflected in the poem. Now how do you connect that, Merrill, with the analysis that you are making? And how do you relate it to the subject matter of the poem in terms of the kind of thing we started off with? Let us take "The Cross." What was the vitality and the reality of that?

MOORE: I think, Bill, that each man would have to try to answer that for himself, and it would take a great deal of thought and soul-searching. I believe that each one of us, in his own way, is trying to do that. I think that Don in his essay, which he read the tail-end of last night, the caudate part, will have a lot to say on it. I think that I could collect a Ransom Omnibus that would be more objective, or more representative, of the real man than your *Selected Poems,* or *Collected Poems;* and I think that Allen can and will do that. You, too, whom I regard as an unpublished poet, because I know you have a large body of unpublished material which I—

ELLIOTT: It will remain unpublished.

MOORE: Well, I don't know about that. But I think that there

the matter of the group splits like the hand splits int
fingers, and the individuals have to try to interpret their ir
dividual rebellion or revolt as each one can do in his ow
way. It certainly admits of the form, a validity to the forr
chosen—I'm guilty of sticking to the most limited form
I've never dared write more than fourteen lines at a time
I think I probably am inhibited from doing so, partly b
habit: I might think something terrible would happen t
me if I did—and I think that Red's perhaps would be th
most interesting and revealing. I always had the feelin
that Red's poems were written right out of the ground an
the rocks and the bushes and the vultures and the image
and symbols of his early life—to which others have bee
added.

ELLIOTT: Yes, but this question of reality and of vitality
you see, had wrapped up in it the whole question of th
well, the levels of reality, of Platonic, or empirical—thes
are very obvious questions.

TATE: I don't think they are specific questions for poetry
Bill. It seems to me that—

ELLIOTT: Well, but if you use the word—forgive me for sug
gesting it—the poet is bound to use words with some cau
tion even when he isn't a poet, when he's a critic.

TATE: Yes.

ELLIOTT: And these words have some leading characteristic
for an inquiry.

MOORE: Well, now, there's a ready-made answer for that, Bill
in the book *The Relativity of Reality* by Réné Laforgue
He says that reality is a relationship between subject an
object. And whether that be a scientist with his cyclotror
or a devout Roman Catholic with his religious milieu, or
psychiatrist and his rats or guinea pigs or conditioned dog
or whether it be a Fugitive on Vanderbilt campus, reactin
to the particularly rich and stimulating environment o
the Fugitive meetings. I always had a feeling that we al

influenced each other; we all rubbed the edges off each other and knocked sparks out of each other in a peculiar way, and that was the so-called mystery, if there is any, to the Fugitive group. There was a peculiar kind of meeting of minds that we had then and we still have, the like of which I have never experienced anywhere else except in this particular circle of human beings.

ELLIOTT: Well, we can all agree on that; and I just want to lay three things on end, and perhaps they will reach scarce nowhere, and then leave them for subsequent development: these words about the nature of poetry and the kind of function that a poet has in his images and in his relationship to whatever you call it—whether reality, or vitality, or any other expressions that you would use for it—have some bearing on the type of rebellion which you've been talking about. A rebellion is against something; but any revolution to be more than a rebellion—and I draw a distinction between the two words—has to have a creative objective. Otherwise, it doesn't continue. Now, what was the creative objective of the Fugitives' rebellion? This is the point. How does it relate to this point?

TATE: [along with an indistinguishable comment by Warren] I'll have to get empirical about this again: the Fugitives' objective was the act of each individual poet trying to write the best poetry possible. I'm afraid we're getting highfalutin again. I just don't—may I speak a little to this point, John, just to something that Red said? It seems to me this test of reality is the test by which we determine whether a given work is poetry or not; and the scale is of importance only after we decide that question, because if we dissolve the poetry into the subject matter, then I think that in the long run—

WARREN: We have a document.

TATE: —we have a document; and what we call the literary tradition is dissolved into its historical flux again. Now take—if I may refer to one of your poems, "Janet Waking," or "Bells for John Whiteside's Daughter." In both of those poems there is a very intense reality which exists in the language, created in the language. That same thing happen in the *Divine Comedy* throughout, not uniformly, but by and large throughout all the hundred cantos. Now we've got there not the difference of reality but a difference of scale. The scale is important only after we decide that difference of reality, or discern that reality. Otherwise we lose the whole conception of literature. It's all gone.

WARREN: May I break in here for a moment? Two things I would string along on what Allen has said about the prior question: it's a question of its existence out of the poem. That's really what I was fumbling at saying. And the other things follow. Another thing: poetry is an exploration; the process of writing is an exploration. You may dimly envisage what a poem will be when you start it, but only as you wrangle through the process do you know your own meanings. In one way, it's a way of knowing what kind of poem you can write. And in finding that you find out yourself—I mean a lot about yourself. I don't mean in the way Merrill's talking about: I mean in the sense of what you can make available, poetically, is clearly something that refers to all of your living in very indirect and complicated ways. But you know more about yourself, not in a psychoanalytic way, but in another way of having dealt with yourself in a process. The poem is a way of knowing what kind of a person you can be, getting your reality shaped a little bit better. And it's a way of living, and not a parlor trick even in its most modest reaches; I mean, the most modest kind of effort that we make is a way of living. And I think Bill has something important when he insists that there is such a thing as a poetic condition, which is the willingness to approach a poem in that spirit, rather than in the spirit of a performer, when you get down to the business of writing a poem, or even thinking about poetry.

TATE: In that sense a man is a poet all the time.

WARREN: All the time, insofar as he brings that spirit into his reading or thinking about poetry or about other things as well. It's a tentative spirit, and a kind of—well, I don't know exactly what's the word, except a lack of dogmatism in dealing with your own responses and your own ideas as they come along, a certain kind of freedom and lack of dogmatism under some notion of a shaping process. The other thing I had to say is more along what Merrill said. I believe that what Merrill, quite properly—now this is again not controversial, but just to make distinction—what Merrill has been talking about deals with the psychology of the process of writing and not with a literary question, at all, it seems to me; that it's a psychological interest that has no bearing on the good poem or the bad poem as such.

ELLIOTT: Yes, that was what I—

WARREN: The bad poem or the good poem could be equally interesting in terms of the way the mind works in creating it, or in the stuff that may call the attention of any of us to the poet himself, or to Merrill Moore—what his psychic history has been. But I can see, I can imagine—this is guesswork, of course—no point-to-point equation between the psychological interest such a process would have from one case to another and the quality of the work that came out of it. That is, the clinicism of it, the clinical interest, would have no relation to the poetic value, necessarily; in fact, it might work the other way.

BROOKS: If I may break in for a moment with an illustration: Hulme makes a point that Rider Haggard's *She* is almost as interesting to the psychologist as—

LYTLE: More so.

BROOKS: —Melville's *Moby Dick,* or perhaps more so.

LYTLE: More so. Yes. May I say something here, in extension to this, or support of it? Red, in this self-exploration, it's both intuitive and deliberate, isn't it? And you may start out with what you think is a subject—say, a subject matter larger than you really end up with, or you can reverse the thing.

WARREN: Yes, you've got to be willing to always shut your eyes and then deal the cards. Just don't look yet.

LYTLE: That's right. And you know Lubbock in *The Craft of Fiction* makes the point that the form, really, uses up all the subject, and the subject all of the form in the ideal situation—

WARREN: In heaven, in heaven.

LYTLE: —in heaven, you see—

TATE: You approach that—

LYTLE: —but you have to approximate that kind of thing, because the subject doesn't exist apart from the words which contain it. But I've been, you know, just thinking how you are going to do it; you think out these things in fiction, of course, not in poetry; and yet there's not such a great difference, I guess. But in this self-exploration there is one danger: if the poet limits it to too close a self-exploration, then it becomes a kind of Narcissistic thing, and you digress, you see.

WARREN: Oh, yes—excuse me. You can't think you are interesting while you are doing it.

LYTLE: No, that's right.

WARREN: You've got to think something else.

LYTLE: Don't you really have to raise against the discrete objects the word, you see?

WARREN: Yes, your self is not involved.

LYTLE: No, that's right.

WARREN: But when you get through you find out that you ate that, too. And of course that—

LYTLE: And when you get these things balanced and related, and sometimes better balanced, sometimes the things that you deliberately work at turn out to be the worst; and sometimes out of that will come a fast-moving blind flash of a page, dialogue, or line, you see. So, in a way, would you say that this was the case: it seems to me that I find times when you look back over it—that is, when you are evolving a thing—that you suddenly discover that there's more there than you thought, finally? And it gives this fresh illumination which makes a further exploration—I mean self-exploration—of the matter in it. Then isn't the body of the work carrying something that is finally mysterious and irreducible to definition?

TATE: If we could reduce it we wouldn't need to write it.

LYTLE: Yes.

STARR: John, may I make a remark here?

RANSOM: Yes.

STARR: All this is enormously interesting to me. We have been listening to poets talking subjectively about the creation of poetry; and it's a rare privilege for all of us who are non-poets. There's no question about that. But to get back to a point that Sidney Hirsch made in which he intimated that the chief criterion of a good poem was subject matter, the loftiness of subject matter. And then Red interposed by saying that the matter of scale would throw him out, and throw a lot of good poets out. And I think maybe they amount to the same thing; not scale in size, because Red used a wonderful phrase in saying what the Fugitives were fleeing from: not only "sweetness and light," but he said "local reference." And that's the key. When John Ransom writes a poem about a small female child's dead pet chicken, it has permanence; and that's the scale—the only scale, I think—against which you can measure the loftiness of subject matter. And I'd like to believe that that's what Sidney Hirsch had in mind when he mentioned subject matter: not the size, or the epic grandeur of the poem, or the significance in human history of it, but that what you were saying has the validity and truth of a permanent value. Now I say that objectively, and I think the non-poet has a right to look for that in any poem, and to measure any poem against that one criterion.

HIRSCH: May I say something? Pardon—were you going to—?

ELLIOTT: I just wanted to get my—

HIRSCH: I was going to say that I think if Mr. Allen Tate would tell us something about how he came to write that poem, "The Maimed Man," and if Donald Davidson would tell us something about how he came to write the poem called "The Demon Brother," and William Elliott would tell us about how he came to write the poem called "Boy's Will Is Wind's Will"—you recall that, William?—and see if they do not throw a great deal of light on the Freudian introduction that Mr. Brooks was talking about. I was thinking about that. I think Hulme throws more light on them than Freud. Do you agree with me?

TATE: Yes.

BROOKS: I, certainly.

LYTLE: I think nearly everybody would agree. I would certainly agree with you.

HIRSCH: And when I consider those three poems, and consider the fact that Mr. Ransom wrote those poems about God—much before he became a member of the Fugitives. You recall, John, that you let me have the manuscripts of those poems two or three years before the Fugitives were formed. I was living in New York, and you sent them to New York. Do you recall that? And I do not believe—may I say this? I possibly should not say it—but I do not think you are as—what shall I say?—as proud of that first book as you are of some of the others.

RANSOM: I have never felt that a poet had any capacity for judging his own poems, and I imagine that not many poets care to make an analysis of their own poems. So I would think my views wouldn't carry very far. It's perfectly true that I didn't like that first volume; that is, I came not to like it: I thought I was doing better ones, but I'm not very explicit.

HIRSCH: You remember the fine poem that Donald wrote about "The Demon Brother"? If that isn't Hulmean, I do not know of a poem that is.

RANSOM: I don't know whether Davidson would care to speak about that point, but we need his voice very much on this general discussion here; I think it's his turn.

DAVIDSON: I thought "The Demon Brother" had been safely buried—it's out of print, and I can't remember how it happened to be written. The only comment I have to make at the moment is that in the poems of my own that I would consider the best, it was not a question of my seizing a subject, but of the subject seizing me.

HIRSCH: May I interrupt; will you excuse me?

DAVIDSON: Yes.

HIRSCH: Isn't that Hulmean right there?

LYTLE: Yes.

DAVIDSON: [along with an indistinguishable remark by Lytle] I don't know anything about Hulme in this; I am not a psychologist at all. Those that I labor the most over are generally the worst—that's not always true, but generally speaking—because as Red says, you have to "wrangle" your way through them; and you may start out with something, and then the poem turns into something else, as in the two new poems that I wrote. One of them started out to be a kind of expression of thanks to a delightful hostess up in Vermont that took Theresa and me in for a while; and then the poem didn't go, and I discovered that really I was writing another poem and had to start over again; and it turned into an entirely different poem. That's all I have to say at the moment, I think.

COWAN: Could it be—

HIRSCH: [*at the same time*] Mr. Tate—Pardon me. Go on.

COWAN: I was wondering if it would be relevant at this point to bring up a topic which you may not wish to comment on. But it strikes me as interesting that the four Fugitives who experimented most with technique and who didn't want to concern themselves so much with subject matter, were the ones who, in 1927, by a rather strange communal reaction, discovered they had a sizable subject matter which they then explored, and which—it seems to me—they made available for other writers.

RANSOM: You must name them.

COWAN: Well, I meant the four Fugitives who later became Agrarians. Is that a topic that would be worth discussing?

RANSOM: I think it's very close to the Fugitives, and a bit of discussion would be quite in order.

COWAN: I don't mean the Agrarian movement proper, but I mean the fact that those four Fugitives—Mr. Davidson, Mr. Ransom, Mr. Tate, and Mr. Warren—found that the subject matter which their poetry had been embodying earlier was a communal subject matter; it was not a private one at all.

TATE: I'm not sure that I understand you. I may be—

ELLIOTT: Well, I think that it's a very interesting point, and it bears directly on what you have said before, and if you will bear with me, I think that it raises a very grave question about the assumption that the poet does search for reality in this self-exploration. And all this effort to create for oneself is, after all, a self in a context.

WARREN: Excuse me, Bill, I didn't mean that—but what happened on the way that could ruin the possibility of a poem.

ELLIOTT: Well, I was agreeing with you about the psychological background, which I thought was entirely correct— that that was not relevant entirely. But the struggle of a man's spirit with his fate, with the circumstances that surround him, with the environment, with the culture, with the traditions that he has around him—this is the essence of the problem. And I believe Mrs. Cowan is asking this question in a somewhat different form: here was an effort to set a tradition and a culture, by some people who became sufficiently conscious of it to think it had a meaning for them in terms of the subject matter which they then transferred over into a different type of exploration. I would like before we turn to the Agrarians just to ask this question: Have we really done justice to the dramatic and the tragic elements in the poet's exploration of reality, the vitality that we are talking about, unless we look for a dimension that modern poets are too often quite willing not to look at? We, quite properly I think, get bored with the Marxians and with the school type of thing that puts everything into a deterministic context, because we repudiate; we cannot feel that this is a pat exploration, and certainly not that pat exploration. I couldn't agree more with people who say that this is an exercise, and a rather trivial one, and won't stand philosophical analysis for any length of time. But, nevertheless, the whole Agrarian rebellion, or revolt, in this group was surely aimed at something that they thought they could correct in the "out-of-jointness" of the times. Now how much did this affect the content of the poems, the reality of the poems? I agree that every poet writes what's in him, that he is seized by the subject matter, as Don has said; this is something older than Hulme. Hulme brings in the "racial unconscious," and I think certainly it may have had some reference to that. This is also a very powerful milieu for poetry, whether it be called a racial unconscious, or cultural tradition, or something of that sort. Do poets really escape this by becoming preoccupied with the dimensions of their own souls in a different context? Doesn't it lead down the road that Proust followed and, to my mind, led him to bankruptcy?

WARREN: And a masterpiece.

ELLIOTT: And a masterpiece, yes, of its sort, too. But I mean it's still a masterpiece of that sort; and it remains embalmed in—

WARREN: We could have a fight about that.

ELLIOTT: Why, sure; we've had a lot of fights: you and I, we are old feuders. But before we fight about it, let's agree on what we are fighting about, and get the thing laid out on end. Don't we have to consider the content, or the tradition, as a part of the poem? And isn't that what Sidney was originally talking about before we raised the Agrarian question, which I hope we will turn to next? I'd like him to have just a final word on what he was leading up to. Those of you who aren't familiar with Sidney's methods will wonder a little bit at this dialectical process, but you mustn't cut it off in mid-stream. Just give him three or four or five minutes, at any rate, to wind up by saying what he was headed at when we were pulled to pieces from several different directions.

HIRSCH: I'd still like to hear, William Elliott, what you have to say about that fine poem of yours, "The Boy's Will Is the Wind's Will."

ELLIOTT: Nobody knows that poem.

HIRSCH: Weren't you interested in Frost at that time?

ELLIOTT: Well, Longfellow was the quotation which I was springing from, but I was thinking from a quite different point of view than Longfellow's "The Wind's Will." The wind has always been a prime symbol to me, because it illustrates in a very definitely poetic form the fate that is impinging on you at all times and that you are wind-blown by.

HIRSCH: Yes.

ELLIOTT: And all poets want to get roots in spite of being wind-blown creatures.

HIRSCH: That's why—

ELLIOTT: Poetry is an attempt at establishing universals which are recognizable. That's the validity of the poem; we all have these conflicts, and they are all generated in various degrees by inner tensions of the psyche. And when we try to translate them into a poem, we have seized on that reality, or that living thing. And that's what a symbol is, if it catches it. Now, is the relevance of the symbol to the subject matter, and that to the tradition and the culture that we are in, a proper measure for judging the importance of poetry? Or can poetry isolate itself?

TATE: Bill, it seems to me that we are talking in two different philosophical languages about the poet here. I don't think that we could follow you—some of us couldn't follow you —when you say the business of the poem is to establish universals. It's to establish the degree in which the universal may participate in the experience, to give it a moment in time; the experience represented by a certain reality of language at a given point. I don't think that poets create universals; they—

LYTLE: —are there to use them.

TATE: Yes.

ELLIOTT: Well, they—

HIRSCH: [at the same time] They discover them.

TATE: Yes. They discover them.

COWAN: —in existence.

TATE: Yes.

ELLIOTT: [*at the same time*]—surely they are attempting to get the most concrete possible expression of them—

TATE: Yes.

ELLIOTT: —this is obvious; but they are still trying to communicate in terms that have varying degrees of meaning to varying people, but have a common character in what I am pleased to call a "universal."

TATE: Wouldn't we part company a little over what you said just then—that the poet is trying to communicate a universal? He's not trying to communicate anything. He's trying to create something real in language.

HIRSCH: What was that again, Mr. Tate?

ELLIOTT: This solipsism puzzles me deeply.

TATE: No, it isn't solipsism; it's Aristotelianism.

ELLIOTT: If he isn't trying to communicate—

TATE: It's Aristotelian empiricism. It's entirely different.

HIRSCH: Is he trying to communicate, did you say? Or is he not?

TATE: Not trying to communicate anything.

HIRSCH: He isn't?

TATE: No, I don't think so. We've got a bad metaphor in the word *communicate*. We've got a wire here; one fellow on one end and somebody on the other end listening to it.

STARR: You said "discover"; that's what he—

TATE: *Discover's* the word.

STARR: To *uncover*—

TATE: *Discover* is a better word.

STARR: But to discover for the reader and for the listener—

ELLIOTT: For whom is he discovering it?

TATE: First, for himself. And if it's not a real discovery, nobody else is going to be able to—

ELLIOTT: True.

LYTLE: Let me say, doesn't he also create his reader, in a sense?

TATE: [*amidst confusion*] Communication means that the person communicating has already got this reader.

ELLIOTT: Don't think he's God. This is an admiration of human beings which poets too frequently share. He can't create his readers or his audience; he can only select that audience and help to create it in the sense that he can communicate into a background that's certainly already there, or there would be no communication.

RANSOM: Couldn't we say that he creates a new experience —that's empirical—a new happiness. He finds, he compounds experiences, or he takes, he's on the verge, he feels an experience; and he stays with it until he realizes the experience. He does it over and over. Other poets akin to him do the same thing. And presently the philosophers will come along, and they are not creative, and they have no existence until the creative people have refined and perfected types of experience. But evidently there is a universal, in the Aristotelian sense, within those—

TATE: Yes.

RANSOM: —experiences, and the wise philosopher can find them out.

TATE: I would have to agree with that. I think that is right.

RANSOM: But that is distinct from the work that the poet does.

WARREN: But you might say their availability depends on

their—let's use this word *depend* a little bit—that their availability depends upon that faculty of the universal; but he is not working in those terms. He's working in quite different terms, and probably even in terms of ideas, ultimately. When Wordsworth was getting along in years, there's a tale I think Crabb Robinson gives, of a clergyman —whose name I think was Miller—calling on him, very reverentially, and telling him while they were taking a walk one morning, "Mr. Wordsworth, I want to tell you how much I admire your poems for their fine morality." And that stumped Wordsworth for a moment; and then he said, "I don't value them for that. I value them for the new view they gave of the world."

RANSOM: Not bad.

WARREN: That's almost the phrasing, not quite. But that's the sense of it—unless I've very badly forgotten the episode —which I think is pretty good. Wordsworth knew what he was up to, I guess.

RUBIN: May I say, parenthetically, that this has been an epoch-making remark: this is the first time I've ever heard any Fugitive admit that Fugitive poetry was in any way influenced by Longfellow.

TATE: I don't think the influence went very deep.

HIRSCH: Well, we heard a great poet say that Longfellow was a great man. Do you remember that, John?

RANSOM: I'm not sure that I do.

HIRSCH: When we took Frost back to the station to catch his train at five o'clock in the morning, he was talking to us about Longfellow and said, "Longfellow was a great poet, a great philosopher, and a great mystic," and that his poems were mystical.

RANSOM: Yes, I do remember.

HIRSCH: Do you recall that?

RANSOM: Yes, I do. I don't think that it's wise of the poet to exclude any other poet, or that poets are in competition with each other, precisely. There are certainly some poets that interest us far more than others—that would mean that we are closer to them—and it might be they would interest philosophers more than other poets, because they've got more fresh material for the philosophers to look at. But I would have the poets that I wanted to read and re-read—it's a big world, and they all have their places. It may be that a poet that doesn't seem fresh to me might be of much more service to his fellow creatures; he might open experience to them far more than I could do in a million years. That would be in terms of some quantitative comparison of the numbers that he would affect. It'd be the only hope of a democratic society, I think: that you've got some spiritual fare for everybody in it. And there are a lot of people that don't know the old fare, the staples of spiritual experience. And then it's proper, I imagine, that there are other poets who are working on the margins of the human experience—of the hitherto explored human experience—and they are making new refinements and finding fresh types of experience of the kind that we call "beautiful"—we have no definition of them. They would all be in their duty in my view.

MOORE: Allen, would it not be what Hart Crane was trying to do when he died? This is more—

RANSOM: Would what be?

MOORE: Exploring a new kind of experience; and projecting, or attempting, to write a kind of epic which due to his short life remained unwritten.

TATE: Well, probably the short life had a lot to do with it; but I think there that we get something that Don referred to a minute ago: when he started out to write one kind of poem and found that he couldn't do it, and the poem turned out to be something else altogether. It began with certain epic features—if you want to use that word—

MOORE: You mean "Lee in the Mountains."

TATE: No, I'm talking about—Don was referring to a new poem that he had done.

MOORE: Oh.

TATE: He'd started to write it in one way, and he found it was a different sort of poem altogether. Well, Crane seems to me to have started "The Bridge" with a consciousness of tension which he couldn't complete; and towards the middle, or past the middle—the section called "The Atlantis" and "Quaker Hill," those two sections—it became something else altogether. By the way, I'd like to say that I don't want Bill to think that I would suppose that the kind of discourse that he's bringing to bear upon the discussion of poetry is not a perfectly good one; but I can't feel that it has much to do with the way poetry originates. It's a perfectly legitimate kind of philosophical discourse after a certain body of literature is in existence—to examine its universals, to examine the implications of its symbolism. But it seems to me at the level of literary studies, that what we are doing there is a kind of historical job. That is to say, it seems to me that no poet would start with a system of symbols held consciously and really discover them as such. He finds that a concrete situation implicates his language in certain symbols as far as the concrete situation will evoke the symbols. And I would say that I think Bill has a Platonic approach to this, while I would think that mine is much more empirical and positivistic, something like that.

ELLIOTT: Yes; well, this goes without saying, and we would have a common ground in our point of diversions. But what I would like to call to your attention—and no more than that—is that the kind of poetry, the kind of symbols, the attention of the poet, the implication that he is drawn in, will depend very largely on the kind of tensions which are created for him. Now, if you are talking about the origins of poetry and the involvement of the poet or if you are talking about the end product of the poem, these are both relevant.

TATE: Yes, they are.

ELLIOTT: And, therefore, what would seem very, very important to you—at a particular moment of your own life, in a crisis of one sort or another—might seem relatively unimportant when you have a culture crisis as profound as the one that we're going through with. And a new school of poetry, for instance, which you doubted we would understand as a group—and I think this is quite likely, because with the perspectives we have now put on, we would have blinders in discovering it—might nevertheless be a perfectly valid type of poetry—

TATE: Of course it would.

ELLIOTT: —and its symbols might have all the elements of reality and vitality because the tragedy that the poet is concerned with is a tragedy of his times and a tragedy of the relationship of the poet to his times and his trying to understand them.

TATE: Well, don't you think we can have a nice concrete example of this sort of thing? From the beginnings of poetry poets have suddenly found themselves in the dark; they've lost their way—in other words, they are in the *colore oscuro*. Now, I'm sure a lot of the Fugitives have felt that way at times; but there's a great difference in the so-called cultural situation between Dante and any of us. Just in the moment he found himself in the dark woods, there was something available to him—a whole cosmos available to him—

ELLIOTT: Right.

TATE: —which is not available to us.

LYTLE: It seems to me, Allen, on this business of symbols— I've been working on a novel that deals with them for about six years now; and what I've discovered is that if you ever take a symbol self-consciously, what you do is force it to perform part of the action, which it cannot do.

TATE: Yes.

LYTLE: Then what you do is to sink yourself into the matrix of the, well, of the interior; and in struggling, trying to get out, you have sunk yourself in a certain way; that what you discover you have happened on is symbols—and I think there are no new ones, that they always repeat themselves in action and nature; and what you find, for example, is the symbol of water, coming out in different implications all the time, showing the enlargement and enrichment of it. You are saying the same thing but in a diverse and enlarged way; so that in the end you get an accumulation.

WARREN: You see the absurdity of that in Malcolm Cowley's *Literary Situation* book, where he goes around complaining about people putting in symbols. Well, many people do, but they are people that he shouldn't be associating with.

TATE: Yes.

WARREN: They're not worth talking about. I mean, what kind of people are you talking about in that whole business about the bad effect of discussions of symbolism? In God's name, who's he been talking to?

LYTLE: Yes.

WARREN: What books has he been reading?

LYTLE: Yes, yes.

HIRSCH: But suppose you consider the symbols just for a moment that Allen Tate, and William Elliott, and Donald Davidson use, which Allen Tate thinks are opposed to the system of symbolism utilized by Dante. Suppose we can show that they were exactly the same symbols—

TATE: Oh, I think there is a relation between them, yes.

HIRSCH: —exactly the same symbol? And Mr. Tate says that he was unaware at the time that they were these universal symbols. You recall, you used the symbols of the pit?

TATE: Yes.

HIRSCH: "There's a pit where some men go; I cannot see the whole of it." Do you recall the rest of it?

TATE: Yes.

HIRSCH: "And the high and transfixed head and heel," and so forth, which has been used by Dante, by a dozen other great poets. Then William Elliott uses the symbol of the wind, and he says it means the spirit. And the wind means the spirit in every language that I know anything about. Doesn't it? You'd thought about that, William, hadn't you? But when you wrote it, you had not, had you?

ELLIOTT: But it means something which blows the spirit, too, to me; this is the difference between the *spiritus* and the *animus* that I was trying to reconcile. And I was influenced by Longfellow only to the degree of trying—if I may set Mr. Rubin right on that—even I, as a member of the Fugitives, was not trying to repeat Mr. Longfellow or gallop the same course with hasty feet—

RUBIN: Of course I thought you were.

ELLIOTT: —but trying to take off from this. And from that point of view the wind has a double symbolism; this is, I think, the subtlety of a poem, if you can manipulate it so as to clarify what you are doing. But it has to have some relationship to a communicable thing that other people are capable of recognizing; that's all I meant.

HIRSCH: I think that word *spirit* is something like a coaxial cable: it has all of these meanings. The first meaning is to turn, to wind around; then compulsion, then—see in the word *spiritus*—spiral—and so forth. Let's see, I wanted to say something else; I've forgot now what it was.

ELLIOTT: We were talking about—

HIRSCH: I was talking about the communication that it makes. I'm sure you've all been seeing and reading about Samuel Beckett's book, something about—what is it, *Waiting for God?*

RUBIN: *Waiting for Godot.*

HIRSCH: *Waiting for Godot.*

STARR: You mean the play?

HIRSCH: Yes.

STARR: *Waiting for Godot,* yes.

HIRSCH: Have you read it?

STARR: Yes.

HIRSCH: Now, he's attempting to communicate something, isn't he? It's as obscure and esoteric as it's possible for a thing to be, but he's attempting to communicate something.

STARR: What?

HIRSCH: Well, I'd like to discuss that with you at another time; but he's communicating something, and he uses terms there which are understandable. Years ago Mr. Ransom and I were having a discussion about something along those lines, and he said, "I see"—do you remember this, John?— "that there is a universal system of symbolism that is in all of the ancient poets." Do you recall that? Universal, always the same—in the *Ramayana,* in the Homeric poems, in Vergil, in Dante. Do you recall our conversation?

RANSOM: Yes.

HIRSCH: Now here is this man using exactly the same symbols, and Tate uses exactly the same symbols; and Tate, at that time, was unaware that he was using them. And that interests me greatly. And I suggest—I venture to say—that's union; just as Davidson did in that poem I mentioned, and

William Elliott in the one called "The Boy's Will Is the Wind's Will." Now, surely in *The Cocktail Party*—which is as obscure as a man can make it—he's attempting to communicate something to somebody, isn't he? That's an attempt at communication; and at this moment—may I say apropos of these universals, or realities—isn't there a reality for the lyric poet? And isn't there another reality for the epic poet? And isn't there another reality for the follower of Polyhymnia? Aren't they trying to do something else? Then, again, isn't the philosopher a poet; and if he isn't a poet, can he be a philosopher? If religion is philosophy allegorized—

RANSOM: He's got to be a very quick man to get far with philosophy; and he has to be very responsive to the fact which is there, which may be a literary fact that's difficult to define; he must have the means of defining it. So there's no possibility of belittling the philosopher. But then neither is he the same man as the man who gave him the materials that he's working with.

HIRSCH: May I suggest—we were speaking of Aristotle a while ago, and Plato. And you recall their definition of poetry. Their definition, if I recall, was that poetry is the passing of non-being into being in appropriate rhythms and terms. Do you recall, Mr. Tate?

TATE: Yes, that would be a good way of putting it.

HIRSCH: Of theogony or cosmogony to cosmology. That's their definition, if you recall, of poetry. Now, therefore, there's one reality for the philosopher and for the religious poet. There's another reality, isn't there, for the lyric poet?

RANSOM: Well, I think that would be very pertinent to the discussion we were having last night, and that's somewhat the conclusion we came to: that the epic poet we were talking about specifically, and the lyric poet, and possibly the dramatic poet, had different interests in mind—different realities appealed to them. And all were in their duty, but they were to be distinguished. In other words, the necessity of distinguishing between people who are related is just as much an obligation, wouldn't you think, as the necessity of relating them, if they are really related?

HIRSCH: And doesn't the gentleman, the philosopher, who does this relating have to be a great poet? These are the most poetic, sensitive, delicate ideas in the world; and if he isn't a great poet, he won't recognize them.

RANSOM: If he has the sense of sameness with difference beyond all other men, I should imagine that the philosopher, because he can articulate more precisely than—

ELLIOTT: He has to package what he says in forms that are like the artifacts of a *poetas,* who is a maker. You know, if you think of Whitehead, who is a very considerable philosopher in our time, and the use of terms which he came upon, like "prehension" and all the organic lingo that he used to convey his ultimate metaphysical ideas, this was sheer poetry—I mean in the sense of symbolism which he had embodied in them. Plato is, by all agreement, I think, a very considerable poet, not only in his myth-making and symbolic characters, but in his architectonic use of forms and in the relationship to each other. Now he is not lyric; I mean, this a different proposition. I think this is what Sidney may be meaning, but I'd rather he'd say so.

HIRSCH: I'm sure that's what I ought to be meaning. [*laughter*]

ELLIOTT: I want you to expound on this bit, if you don't mind.

HIRSCH: I think when Plato says, and Aristotle quotes him, that the poet has to express non-being passing into being, in appropriate rhythms—I forget his exact language, but rhythms, and meter, and appropriate and lofty language, and so forth—he is describing a great poet there. Do you recall, Mr. Ransom?

RANSOM: I think so.

HIRSCH: He says he has to be the greatest of poets. In fact, he says, he's the only poet he would allow in his ideal Republic. And so ontologically, I'd suggest that it be considered that there's a reality—which is *paradeigma,* isn't it, the paradigms, the ideas that inhabit the realm of thought? And he calls them *ethos,* if you recall: the proper theme for a poem, he says, the proper theme for a poem. I hesitate to say that, but I suppose you recall the word is a synonym for Dionysus.

STARR: Well, it may be—it may well be—that the great poet consciously uses the lofty language and the symbolism that characterize these permanent values and is easily recognized thereby; and that the minor poet occasionally reaches greatness by unconsciously using these same symbols that give permanence. But one thing is certain: the poem, like the drama, its value is shock value—dramatic value—to the reader, the listener, the audience. And it's the value of recognition. In a sense the poet doesn't create at all—no matter what he digs out of himself, or what implements— he re-creates.

LYTLE: That's right.

STARR: And he re-creates something in his own way, in his own particular style, which when communicated—because if it isn't communicated, it is nothing at all; if there's no audience, it might as well be a blank page. But he communicates something that has the shock value on the listener, the value of recognition. Now if the listener or the audience is going to recognize this, then it has to be something profoundly and deeply universal and permanent.

WARREN: May I nag this communication business again, just a little bit? If a thing is made right, it's going to be available to a lot of people—if it's made right. But you can't make it right by thinking of those people.

LYTLE: That's right, that's right.

WARREN: You see what I'm getting at. I think you are trying to find the principles of creating that object somehow, out of what? I mean, you are bound to be in there somehow; but you cannot take it from the side of the communications. It's going to communicate: you create the thing, and there it sits on the mantelpiece, or wherever it is—

LYTLE: Red, that's what I meant when I said—

WARREN: —and then everybody can look at it. And if it's made right, it's going to signify, so that we can all look at it.

STARR: Well, Red, you are talking—

WARREN: It'll make us all feel something significant, big or little. But what you have to keep your mind on is making that "thing." And making it significant to me would not make it significant to somebody else. Working at the object is finding the laws of that object that you are working with.

LYTLE: Yes. If you think of anything outside of the thing that you are doing, you are lost. You can't do it; you'll never do it.

WARREN: It's all right to think about whether it's going to be in it or not. [*laughter*] But that doesn't matter. You see what you get.

HIRSCH: Could I say something there? Don't you think that Samuel Beckett, when he wrote *Waiting for Godot,* using certain obscure and esoteric symbols which are known to very few—and he obviously wanted to communicate something—he had in mind those who would receive and accept and recognize those symbols? And he knew that's a tribe that is very seldom met with, and when they're met with, they are very few.

LYTLE: Let me say this on that, if I might, Mr. Hirsch: if he got the action right, it would represent the symbol; then it would be available.

HIRSCH: They seek in every way to avoid action. Have you noticed there's no action in *The Cocktail Party?*

WARREN: I found it out most disastrously. [*laughter*]

HIRSCH: There's absolutely no action. It's tedious and tiresome.

MOORE: May I, Mr. Hirsch—

HIRSCH: While sitting in the theater, I saw that half the audience was sound asleep. *The Cocktail Party,* and the other one—what was the other one, by Fry? *Venus Observed?*—I saw. They made every effort to avoid action, and may I suggest that in itself is a communication?

LYTLE: Well—[*to Moore*] Go ahead.

MOORE: This will keep; go ahead.

LYTLE: Well, all I was going to say was that you take the dragon fight, which is an action representing one of the universal symbols, you see, as old as the hills, reinterpreted from time to time. At the same time, it is first an action; you may not understand the symbolic reference—you may be able to understand it intuitively, but it is first an action and the action contains it. You see it in Andromeda when she is rescued, for example.

HIRSCH: May I tell you something? I went to see *The Cocktail Party* two or three years ago in New York, and I went with a very interesting and highly cultured European lady. And I went with a third party, a very noted psychiatrist. We could not get the three seats together. The lady and I sat together; the psychiatrist sat in another part of the theater. After the first two acts—she was a very interesting person, very cultured European filly, usual German culture, you know, who knew Goethe and Schiller, and who made pilgrimages to Goethe's place, and so forth—and after two acts of it, she turned to me and said, "I'm frankly bored. I find it terribly tedious. Let's go." I said, "I feel exactly the same way." But we were to meet the psychiatrist in the lobby of the theater. Then the third act came on, and suddenly there were four or five lines that were so startling I said, "Listen to this, now; listen to these lines! Listen! Watch!" Afterwards we went into the lobby of the theater and the psychiatrist came up and said, "For God's sake, did you hear those lines? Did you hear those three or four lines?" The man had utilized the entire play as a vehicle in order to put across the two or three lines.

MOORE: May I—

HIRSCH: And I—Go ahead, Merrill, I just—

MOORE: After you.

HIRSCH: —wanted to say if you and I, or Allen Tate or William Elliott or Alfred Starr or Donald Davidson, if we were together and watched that play—Mr. Lytle—and these lines came up—

MOORE: Well, now, I had a chance to talk to Mr. Eliot about that play, and I want to tell you what he said. This was when he came up last year, I believe it was, to give the talk for the *Advocate*. First of all, we had heard that he had written this play before it was produced. And a friend of mine, Jed Harris, read the play before it was produced and said, "It's a poor play, and I won't produce it." But it was put on in the United Kingdom somewhere—in the summer theater?

STARR: Edinburgh.

MOORE: And did pretty well? Then it came here, and it made a great hit. But I asked Mr. Eliot about it, and he said, frankly, that the play was a vehicle for certain ideas that he had gotten from the Greeks; that he put it in the modern cast because he thought it would be sensational, because of the popular fallacy of putting all on psychiatry, that he thought it would be fashionable to put it into a psychiatric setting, but that the basic ideas concerned ideas remote from the central plot. And he considered one of the most important figures the woman who went off and got herself crucified—

HIRSCH: In an anthill.

MOORE: —in an anthill, and that she was a very important character, and that she didn't even appear, but was only casually mentioned in some of those lines that you speak of. I think Mr. Eliot was using his art consciously—and almost cleverly—to get his ideas across. And I'd agree with you, Sidney, on that; and I believe Allen would, too, if we could have the play here. But this is what strikes me as equally important: I believe that John Ransom's series of twenty sonnets, *Two Gentlemen in Bonds*—about the two brothers, and the peach and the sister and the property, and the brother who liked to sleep, and the brother who liked to eat, you know, who couldn't put on weight and the one who got—

STARR: Talk into the mike.

MOORE: —who got fatter all the time—I think that what we need beside the creative artist is a promotive artist and that a really good—well, a man like Red could take that and rewrite it, using Ransom's ideas, for script, and produce a very fine two-hour or four-act or three-act play out of your sonnets. Now—

WARREN: Well, I bet you that neither one of us would agree to it. [*laughter*]

RANSOM: I'll turn it over to you, Red; I'll pay you to take it. [*laughter*]

WARREN: Keep it the way it is.

MOORE: Now, let me finish—

WARREN: I don't want to murder it up.

MOORE: It's quite in line with what Mr. Somerset Maugham

said about his play, *Rain*. He said he wrote a short story called "Rain," or "Sadie Thompson," or something, and forgot about it. And then two young fellows came up and said, "Mr. Maugham, will you let us put this into a play? We think it's a good story and would reach a wide audience." And it was his first hit. And thereafter he wrote others which were well known. I believe that we, last night or in the previous meetings, approved one thing: in starting this group we were running away from something. We were negatively motivated. But when we got going, we didn't know where to go; so we stopped. Now, maybe that's heresy; maybe I'm wrong. But I wonder if you, Alfred, would pick it up and restate your thesis of yesterday evening, if you wish, and carry the torch a little farther?

BROOKS: May I break in at this point to ask Alfred if he will take out the tablets of his memory, note this, put it down to start us next time, because I've been asked to stop us promptly at four. I think that this might be a fine transition. I, for one, would like to see the matter come up—

WARREN: It's a good beginning for an obituary, anyway. [*laughter*]

STARR: At any rate, I'm very happy that we have completely exhausted one subject, that one that Mrs. Cowan asked about. And now we know all about how the Fugitive poets, shall we say, degenerated into the Fugitive-Agrarians. [*laughter*]

DAVIDSON: I don't agree to that at all. Mrs. Cowan's question was not answered. [*laughter*]

BROOKS: Don, don't you know irony when you hear it? [*laughter*] The question will be answered in our next session.
[*general murmur*]

FOURTH SESSION

Saturday Morning, May 5

Moderator: CLEANTH BROOKS

BROOKS: One thing that I want to remind you of: it seems to me, an obviously prejudiced witness, but trying to be objective, that the talks have gone wonderfully well. All sorts of highly interesting things have gotten themselves said. I think that all of us probably are aware of the fact that occasionally the discussion ran out into the sand in a few places. All that I would like to remind you of today is that there are lots, still, of highly important topics that I think some of us would like to hear you talk about. I don't want to push us away—I, surely, least, I hope, of any in the room—from the discussion of poetry. On the other hand, the situation of the poet in relation to culture, in relation to the South, in relation to the whole concept of community, those seem to me terribly important things about which all of the Fugitives have written or acted and continue to write and act. I wonder whether Andrew might throw the ball out that way, and if it's not accepted, well, then somebody will throw out another ball.

LYTLE: Which ball do you want me to throw out here?

BROOKS: Well, any of the sift that I've spread out on the table.

LYTLE: Well, I was just wondering, as far as a practicing

poet is concerned, about the poets who became Agrarians—the Fugitives who became Agrarians; actually, aren't we making a false distinction to divide them too explicitly into segments? It seems to me in this first stage, when they were trying to purify the word in terms of poems and discussion, their flight was from that spurious word which defined the cultural tradition and its history, and that historical circumstance of the First World War, which gave this affluent kind of release into which all things seem to be extravagantly enlarged. Then suddenly, as always, you come back to the domestic scene, into the local situation; and the trial at Dayton focused it—as a concrete instance always does. And then what you got was the poet operating at various levels of interest, which is certainly an ancient and long standing kind of procedure. To me it is a false distinction to say that one thing ended and another began, when actually it was a kind of continuation. That would throw the ball.

MOORE: May I debate that question, brother Lytle? I think its extemely important, in view of what John Crowe Ransom has brought out in the example of Yeats, to make that distinction and to make it very sharply. There were two distinct movements, even though one grew into another; and the members of the Fugitives who went into the Agrarian group were four, I believe, or five maybe?—but the greater majority of the Fugitive group was not interested in the Agrarian movement, or the Neo-Agrarian movement; and I, for one, would strongly emphasize that fact. And there is a confusion throughout the country that the words *Fugitive* and *Agrarian* equate, which is not true at all. And I think we ought to start off by making it very clear that there was a literary movement; then out of it grew another movement which might be called "quasi-political," to use John Ransom's phrase. And I took occasion last night to look up the life of Yeats and read it; and after I read about sixty pages, I came to the conclusion that John's example to us—or his warning to us—could be taken two ways: either that Yeats should have remained the contemplative man and should not have tried to please his unattainable ladyfair and could possibly have written a poem approaching epic dimensions, or he should have gone into politics. I feel that neither the poet helped the politician very much, nor did the politician honor the poet very much; but, as Mr. Ransom said, he had to "coarsen" his poetry to participate in politics. And I'd like to throw that hunk of beef into the stew for what it may be worth.

LYTLE: But isn't a writer, isn't the poet—he's not a politician; I mean, he writes in terms of his medium. And, of course, when he writes critically, he writes as a man of letters and not as a politician; not as a historian either, you see. I want to make that distinction: that it's a continuous kind of operation of the same kind of mind growing into a different kind of air.

MOORE: I don't believe it's the same kind of mind; I think it's a very different kind of mind in terms of the ego structure that's been defined by others more able than myself. I think the poet is much more akin to the philosopher than the politician; and I believe that poets make poor politicians, generally speaking.

LYTLE: Well, there was no political action on the part of this.

MOORE: No, but it had great political implications.

LYTLE: Why, certainly, the same as every act.

TATE: I liked John's evocation of Yeats as a kind of model of what we might have been; but I think that the circumstances of Yeats and the circumstances we found ourselves in were very, very different. Ireland is a country with the area of the state of Kentucky, almost exactly. It has four times as many people in it. There's an ancient and homogeneous culture, much more homogeneous than the Southern culture. And it didn't have to operate through a complicated political machinery, the Free State, as we operate through the government in Washington. Our whole political organization in this country by states would make it very difficult for us to function as Yeats did. You see, no poet could have played the dual role in this country as it was possible for Yeats, "A.E.," and several other people in the Irish Renascence. Now another thing that I would like to argue a little bit with John about: I can't believe Yeats coarsened his language; I think he made it much more subtle and plainer. It was near a prose diction, but much more subtle and much richer. If we compare "The Wanderings of Oisin" with one of Yeats' later poems, like "Among School Children," the language has been immensely enriched. He had developed a theory of the "bomb-line"; you write eight prose lines, then you put an atom bomb in the ninth that explodes the whole thing. He was a great composer. Well, all that is a little beside the point, but I think—

ELLIOTT: No, it's right on the point, absolutely.

TATE: Yes. But I do think that as poets, that is, there were four—weren't there four of us, or five, who went over from the Fugitive phase into the Agrarian phase?

ELLIOTT: There were four.*

TATE: Yes. I can't agree it was a different sort of mind, given the particular cultural situation that we find ourselves in since the end of the eighteenth century. You know the literary critic doesn't turn on a different mind; it's a different mode that he's operating in. And if I may modestly refer to myself, I would say that some of the best verses I have written—if I may use the word "best"—I did during the Agrarian phase in the 1930's—

* Ransom, Davidson, Tate, and Warren.

BROOKS: Don has asked to—

TATE: —and I just don't see this complete division.

BROOKS: —asked for a chance to speak at this point. Suppose we—

DAVIDSON: Well, I would completely agree with Allen as to the difference between the Irish situation and ours, in the first place, and in general as to Yeats, though I've never been certain—absolutely certain—that Yeats took the right line, but that's another question; that's a critical question. I would also agree with Allen's point that they are not different types of mind, and I would say that the symposium *I'll Take My Stand* can be taken just as much as a defense of poetry as it can be taken as a defense of the South—

TATE: I agree with you.

DAVIDSON: —or of any particular politics, or economics, or anything. The general point is—in that book—that in the order of life that we would defend or seek to establish, these things are not to be separated if life is to be healthy at all; that the separation of them into specialties under the modern regime is the thing, above everything else, that destroys poetry. Therefore, *I'll Take My Stand* is as much a defense of Merrill Moore as a poet, and of Bill Elliott as a poet, and as a student of government—a free student of government, not bound under a totalitarian regime—it's as much that as it is an exposition of the case of the South under the Agrarian conception.

TATE: Don, I think that's very good, because it seems to me what we were doing—

DAVIDSON: Yes. I have one more point to make. Now it'd be an error, I think, for Merrill to imply, as he seems to be implying, that his poems at present have no political context; because I would argue that they do have a political context, and he can't get away from it. He can't escape into some sort of walled compound and say, "Now, I'm a poet when I'm here, you see, but in this other compound that I'll go over into, now I'm a psychiatrist; and then if I go into public affairs, that's still another compartment." It's true that the modern world tempts you to do that, but that's an illusion.

MOORE: I admire you for saying that—

DAVIDSON: Yes.

MOORE: —your neo-political implications are as much a defense of the individual poet as they are of the individual government. But I would correct you by saying, that if my poems are political, I am not aware of it; and if they are political, I would shade the word by saying they are more sociological than political. Now I have had a long correspondence—

DAVIDSON: That exactly is the point; that is what I am talking about: sociology *is* politics, now, Merrill.

MOORE: No, it is not politics. The sociologists do not say so.

DAVIDSON: I know they don't say so, but we all feel the effect of their political activity.

MOORE: Well, now pardon me for being so—

DAVIDSON: What do you suppose the great uproar is about in the South right now?

MOORE: Well, it's about a lot of things, including anxiety.

RUBIN: Let's stay in the 1920's.

DAVIDSON: Well, now, the effort to psychoanalyze the South as if it were a patient stretched out on the—

TATE: "Etherized" is what—[*laughter*]

DAVIDSON: —ether couch—

THORP: Not etherized.

DAVIDSON: —that just simply won't work, because they're

not going to submit, Merrill. That's all there is to it; you can't get them into your clinic. [*laughter*]

TATE: Now, let me make a point here, before we go on. I have a little more to say. I would interpret Don's view of *I'll Take My Stand* when he says it's a defense of poetry as—

DAVIDSON: I said it's as much that as anything else.

TATE: Yes, yes. I think there was an underlying assumption to which we would all subscribe, and short of the political implications, I think Merrill would subscribe to, too. We all assume that a kind of religious humanism is the moral and spiritual condition which is favorable to poetry. And the cutting edge of the book seemed to be historical and po- litical, but the thing that gave the book value to me, and still gives it value—and, as a matter of fact, gives it value to readers elsewhere besides the South, even today—is what I would call the reaffirmation of religious humanism, and that is very intimately connected with poetry.

RUBIN: Allen, don't you think it's a metaphor—the book, *I'll Take My Stand,* is really a metaphor?

TATE: Well, yes, of course it is, yes. What do you mean pre- cisely?

RUBIN: Well, I mean primarily it's a large figure—

TATE: Yes.

RUBIN: —worked at by poets, and I think there were about twelve of them—

TATE: Yes.

RUBIN: —and that was the primary use of it; and in so saying, I'm not in any way running down—

ELLIOTT: Well, that doesn't really come to grips, I think, with the problem. I think Merrill—if he will forgive me for intervening for a moment, playing the role as moderator, and as pacificator—has made a very important point, and I guess there was something in what Donald was saying that would lead him to that kind of separation. Pure poetry—or some idea that there is a pure poetry—and coarsened poetry is inherent in the sort of split that's been very deep in this group from the beginning; and we assumed different phases. I happen to share very deeply a view that Andrew Lytle, Allen Tate, and Donald Davidson have just made: that the poet is a part of his times—I was trying to bring that out yesterday: that really the new tragedy of the poet is, in a very large dimension, the tragedy of his setting and his times and that he responds to it. I think that deeply embedded in the whole Fugitive movement was an attempt to flee *from* something, and then when they fled a certain distance to flee *toward* something, to get back to a South that they felt was a right tradition in the nation—

DAVIDSON: Almost like Toynbee's "Withdrawal and Return," you see.

ELLIOTT: Well, this is not just Toynbee; this is a very old conception. And if I may speak a word about Yeats without offense to you, I lived just across the street from Yeats; we had him in at these long all-night sessions; we had special permission—unique in an Oxford college, so far as I know —to let him out the postern gate at any hour of the morning; and nobody else ever had that, that I know, in an Oxford college. And I spent hours in his library talking mysticism and the things that he was most interested in; and Yeats essentially and deeply was a mystic. If you will read the translations from *The Upanishads* and things of that sort that he was concerned with, he never lost this. Talk to old —what's the boy's name, in the—

MOORE: "A. E."?

ELLIOTT: "A. E." I spent equal time with "A. E." in Dublin; I have thirty-page letters from him. And "A. E." was the great interpreter of the national being; he was deeply embedded in this thing. But the question is what was the relation of the poet to the man of vision about politics? Yeats couldn't have written "Kathleen ni Houlihan," not just addressed to Maud Gonne. This was deeply embedded in his effort to recreate some sort of myth for the Irish of their past, and things of that sort. And there I would diverge a little from Allen, if he doesn't mind, by saying that actually the ingredients of Yeats are not foreign to the ingredients of the Fugitives, that the cultural tradition—now there sociology does play a part in politics; it's the matrix of politics; it is politics in the Aristotelian sense of politics, embracing this whole concept of politics, which is man's relation to his community.

WARREN: That's not sociology, Billy—

ELLIOTT: No, I say—

WARREN: That's the material which sociology is claiming to deal with.

ELLIOTT: Exactly. I'm just claiming it for politics in the sense that I profess politics. I went over into professing politics precisely for this reason, and the books I have written, like *The Pragmatic Revolt* and a long string of others, have been, I hope, infused with some poetic sense of symbolism, with myths and the interpretation of myths, and—to whatever degree I could carry over into it—with some of the insights that a poet has to have. Now, the point I want to wind up with is this: that, if you take what the Fugitives were doing in the Agrarian movement—though we split as to its complete meaning—we, all of us, went along, I think, with this offense against the Yankee invasion that was, so to speak, overwhelming our country with a commercialism and a withdrawal from the values which in the South had always moderated these things. These values had given the South those Aristotelian virtues, that Johnny taught us from the beginning, of the "Athenian Gentleman"—that was his expression for Aristotle, and I have never forgotten it. These things did put some measure and some limits on the drives that were purely repetitive; and we didn't, on the other hand, swing over to the Marxian panaceas, the magic formulae by which the world was to be set right through some Jewish minor prophets, or through lucubrations of the British Museum on what made the world and the universe tick, derived from studies of the Greek atomists, the materialists. We did attempt to restate, and in our various ways all subscribed in different degrees to the things that the Agrarian movement was trying to get at. You threw me out, more or less, for my feeling that our myth had to be a myth capable of meeting the Nazi myth, the Fascist myth at that time, or the Russian myth, you see; and that those required power as an ingredient, that poets have to come to some grips with the realities of power, with the things that move men, with the basic source of strength. But that leads us right back into this affirmation of values which we cannot escape, and which poetry is in some sense infused with very deeply. Don has felt so passionately about that that it has given a whole impelling character to his life. And we may differ—and it is appropriate to differ—about the directions and the degrees of the symbols that we are applying to politics and the ways which they may take. I always thought that Agrarianism's chief virtue was to retain the gentleman, if you like—to retain a tradition. I don't find in Virginia today, in practicing farming, that that life produces the kind of thing we hoped the South stood for. It's in a different context: the world market sets all sorts of things; the prices of machine products are controlled— as against the uncoordinated nature of our whole agricultural processes. This is a thing that has to be studied by people who devote their lives to it, too. But a poet's insights into the things that are behind that, and a poet's affirmation of the values that should be used to govern, were the things that I thought the *I'll Take My Stand* boys were concerned with. When Andrew Lytle dredged up out of the history of Tennessee the dog-trot, and the kind of life that a man could live who could live like a gentleman on his holdings, and work hard at it but still not be completely obsessed by it, he was affirming something that might relate to our businessmen, like Jesse Wills and Alfred Starr. When you can find businessmen controlled by this kind of a feeling, you have something that moderates and chastens the nature of American civilization. And if the poet can infuse that quality into it, if he can get into it the concepts once again—concepts that are bigger than mere repetitiveness, or mere advertising, or the horrors of the impact of television on us today, and every other form of incitement to spend—then he has performed a role as a poet by capturing the imaginations of people and leading them back to other models. And this I think, is a function of poetry that poets can never escape, and that they always in some degree affirm, whether consciously or unconsciously. Merrill is limiting himself because he concerns himself with the particular problems that he feels best able to reflect, and there's no reason he shouldn't. This is a very deep area of human behavior and of human life, and has to be understood. But it isn't the limit of a poet. When Red Warren translates into other vehicles, and into the kind of poetry that he put into *Brother to Dragons,* the interpretation of all, the whole panorama of politics; when he writes about the King's M— you know—

RUBIN: *All the King's Men.*

ELLIOTT: —*All the King's Men,* he is essentially a poet projecting his values on the scheme and trying to recall people to them. I have a very much more affirmative nature than you do. I'm always looking for more remedies. I'm not just a diagnostician, though I've spent my life diagnosing, too. And that is also a realm in which a poet can operate. Sometime before we break up I want to read you a poem about the thing that I am gripping with in the Security Council, about the nuclear fission problem, about the impact of that on humanity. This is something I am seized with: it comes out of my bad dreams at night.

MOORE: Read it now.

ELLIOTT: No, it's not appropriate to read it now. I beg leave to carry this discussion on and get back to the—

TATE: Read it to us at lunch.

ELLIOTT: Maybe that's a good time to do it; and I'd be glad to get your help with it as to whether or not this is mixture of the genre. In other words what I've said, or tried to say, is that poetry can operate in all media; and Johnny was reminding us of that. Poetry that's appropriate to one medium, to one set of stuff, will not be appropriate to other sets. A lyric poem, a love poem, a poem that you write to your love or to your friends is of an order of experience more intimate and, therefore, different; but it's infused with the same sort of values that are against totalitarianism; it's that you never use a friend—you know, all the things that go along with love, and loyalty, and friendship. But, on the other hand, there's nothing whatever to prevent poets—if they are able to do it—from moving in this medium or another, and from drawing from their experience and insights as poets in the fictional medium. I thought that had been the common conclusion, if there were one, that we reached about the relations of fiction to poetry.

MOORE: Well, now, could I ask one question or lay one ghost, if I may, because I think it's a silly ghost and I don't want it tagged in these records. Our good friend and brother, Donald Davidson, spoke of anyone wanting to psychoanalyze the South. That's ridiculous; the South is not sick. The South is alive, healthy, well, growing, and struggling; and if the South were to be psychoanalyzed, it would take two couches, Don, because there are two Souths, and—

DAVIDSON: More than two.

MOORE: More than two? More than two couches?

RANSOM: Tens of psychiatrists.

MOORE: [laughing] That's right. It would take a Fugitive reunion to do it.

ELLIOTT: And then we would psychoanalyze the psychiatrists. [laughter]

MOORE: That's right. But I'd like to ask this of John Ransom: he spoke to us last night in a parable about William Butler Yeats, and that parable has been continued today by one who knew Yeats; and I would like to know if this is not implied in your parable: that the poet has the choice to decide whether he remains a poet or whether he becomes a politician, and, if so, is not that the point whereon the Fugitive rock split, or the Fugitives debarked, decamped, and then went into another—I believe someone called it last night—reincarnation? And if it can be determined, when did that point occur? Was it with the closing out of *The Fugitive*, the periodical published from '22 through '25, or when was it? Would you care to comment on that John?

RANSOM: Well, I'd like to go beyond that. You know, Fugitives are pretty tough guys, and when my point is resisted, the whole implication for me is to study it pretty hard and see what's there and especially with a view to finding that something is there.

BROOKS: May I break in—just at this point, John, to load you with more material, because I would like to suggest— much as I hate to differ with you—that your account of Yeats seems to me just dead wrong.

MOORE: I felt that, too.

BROOKS: Maud Gonne wanted him to be a politician, and he couldn't use dynamite; in fact, he scolds her for wanting to use—

RANSOM: I don't think you can define a politician as a man that's going to use dynamite. [laughter]

BROOKS: Okay, maybe not. My point is—

WARREN: A man who is willing to in the end, though—

BROOKS: Anyway, let me throw this in as you talk to us on the matter: that there would be a good deal of evidence that Yeats actually gave up the heroes, gave up the epic, and giving up Maud Gonne, turned to the inner man and became the great poet that we know later, which would be a way of getting back to Andrew's point: there isn't any real split here.

ELLIOTT: Well, we can differ about that. I meant to say Ezra Pound when I was talking a while ago, because talking with old Pound and talking with the people that reconstruct in this period, Pound's influence on Yeats as a poet was absolutely enormous—

TATE: T. S. Eliot, too.

ELLIOTT: T. S. Eliot, yes. The two of them had a very great impact, but we could go into that and discuss Yeats—

TATE: But, Bill, isn't there—

ELLIOTT: Let Johnny talk.

TATE: Excuse me. What you are talking about began long before the late nineteenth century. Milton didn't turn on a different mind when he wrote the *Tracts*—

ELLIOTT: That's what I was trying to say—

TATE: Yes—

ELLIOTT: —the other day.

TATE: —and I suppose he was the first great poet—

ELLIOTT: [*at the same time*] We must let Johnny get back—

BROOKS: Yes, I didn't want to divert him from that; I just wanted to feed more material for the hopper.

ELLIOTT: Excuse me for interrupting; we'll continue this later.

RANSOM: Well, I promise not to be too long. But, now, Allen, did I understand you correctly when you were introducing that last reading of yours—*

TATE: Yes.

RANSOM: —to say that you hoped but scarcely expected to finish that poem?

TATE: Well, I—

ELLIOTT: If you don't, I'll haunt you.

TATE: Well, how can anybody expect anything, John?

RANSOM: Well, then you are involved—

TATE: [*at the same time*] It's just a question of hope.

RANSOM: Now, I am heavily involved. I never go anywhere but what people say, "Why did you leave poetry and go to criticism?"

TATE: Yes.

RANSOM: I expect others of you have the same experience. And I say, "Well, it's a free country." That's the easiest answer. [*laughter*] I have never been happy with the thought that I had left poetry. I've continued to make threats of writing more poems; I even still do. But I am very much concerned with the thing that we have scarcely considered because it came from the enemy camp. Mencken used to say that everybody has got a little volume of verse that he did at eighteen years old; but he goes to prose when he grows up and he's mature. Now, I should say that poetry is a much bigger and more versatile—well, leave out the "bigger"—it's a much more versatile and comprehensive instrument than we give it credit for being. And I think of some poets who continued with poetry, like Wordsworth, when they might as well have stopped poetry. I'm thinking

* A reference to Tate's reading of "The Swimmers" at the Friday night poetry-reading.

of poets that continued: Dryden continued as a satirist and playwright, and I, for one, don't like the eighteenth century satire; I don't think it's one of the highest modes of poetry. It's very personal and venomous, but it was a fighting mode. And then the playwright can always go on. And then I think I introduced the other evening the idea that fiction is a very creative and noble instrument which has some kinship with poetry—the kind of fiction which I like—and we don't have to compete with that. But I think that of all poets, Yeats did more to keep on with poetry, and, in fact, to some extent, the late poems are like a second childhood and suffer from some of the defects of a second childhood which I hope no Fugitive will ever lapse into. But at the same time, it was a very great problem there, and I figure a poet conceivably as a man who grows up in an art which is quite wide enough to take him in. And there are countless brilliant phrases of Yeats which are comments on affairs, and the comments on the wrong turn that a beautiful woman might take by plunging into politics and hatred and violence. And there are many comments in Yeats—and sometimes there are whole little poems—which seem to me perfect, which seem admirable; and they have great political implications. I must say here, though, that as for myself I think it's later than Brother Elliott thinks and later than Don thinks. I think that we are faced—

DAVIDSON: You don't know what I think. [*laughter*]

TATE: Well, we'll hear that in a minute.

RANSOM: I know, Don. I know that there's a creative streak in you that tames a lot of things that I wouldn't think tameable. But my feeling is that we are faced with a new culture in this country, that the strings that bound us to Europe are all gone. Anybody who teaches English knows that the Department of English goes down steadily and proportionately in the appeal which it makes to students. I introduced into my house—or rather my son did before I knew it, almost—a television set last summer. [*laughter*] I use it to go slumming. And I must confess that I think it's very healthy that we are starting all over here in this country with a kind of culture which is based on mass consumption. And on the political side, while we have people that oppose the New Deal, I should say that the manufacturers and the bankers in the long run will have to keep the New Deal, that they are fooling with economic dynamite if they propose to cancel it. And I would go even further than that and say that the great patron of our times is St. John the Baronet, that is St. John Maynard Keynes; and that his economy is the only one that will continue capitalism in operation. That's incidental; I don't welcome that at all. But it does make me say that I think that we can't have any effect on the economy, and that what results is that humanism is a way of life; and the people who practice it might as well call it a metaphysical society or a mode of life; that it's a minority group, and it can even be operated by people who are thoroughly attuned to the new economy, because that's the only thing that saves us. It happens that at my college now there's in preparation, under the presidency of the President and the committeeship of some people of like mind with his, an attempt to revive the whole humanism of Babbitt; and they are going to have a great conference next spring in which the cards are stacked, and they'll get humanists to speak on the economy, on politics. And I have said to them that that's a metaphysical society, that that place doesn't belong in the platform of any party; and if you come into power, you would immediately have to cancel your platform and deal with the newer forces that actually work in our economy. And I don't mean that the poet in this economy could do even what Yeats wanted to do. He could have an effect on the forces of politics, which are economic forces; but he could make himself known, I think —could make his point known—very effectively, if he extended the line of his poetry: philosophical, satirical images —the images of people which are very powerful in Yeats.

And I think it would be very refreshing and ennobling to the general discussion. Allen, you've said in a poem that this is an age in which "whores are delinquents." And that was a wonderful line of satire which you started, and I think the best satire in English, the best mode of satire that I'd ever seen in English. And, at the same time, I don't think the lyric impulse should be forgotten. But I imagine that as Fugitives we cultivated mostly the lyrical impulse, and that we couldn't extend it to cover the affairs that we now wanted to treat. And I think we stopped too soon, perhaps. I want to study that and—

TATE: You began your very illuminating talk by referring to the fact that you are frequently asked by friends why you gave up poetry. Now, I don't think you gave it up, if I may say so. All poets differ; there's a certain period of life—and it doesn't confirm Mencken's notion about that— in which people write. Thomas Hardy was able to write poetry up until he was past eighty. But it seems to me that when we approach the matter this way, there's a concealed analogy, an evolutionary theory [*murmurs*] that the poet has got to develop, you see. Well, poetry doesn't develop. In a poet like T. S. Eliot, his range becomes greater, but he's no better in *The Four Quartets* than he was in *Gerontion;* in fact, I think *Gerontion*'s the most original poem he wrote, and the most powerful.

RANSOM: Well, Allen, I don't have any biological analogy in mind, I think, but in our experience we developed; and undoubtedly we extended the range—

TATE: Yes, yes, that's true.

RANSOM: —for ourselves.

TATE: Yes, yes.

RANSOM: And that's my point, that we—

DAVIDSON: That's all right as long as you don't use it with

the evolutionary and metaphorical meaning that Allen referred to.

TATE: But what I had in mind was this: that I would like to see you write a great deal more poetry. But if your poetry stopped, say, ten years ago, it's a fact that we can't question or even explore. It would be fatal, I think, for any of us—not only John but any poet—to say, "Now I've got to write poetry to meet a certain cultural situation with its political and economic implications." All poets differ, all poets differ—

RANSOM: No, that isn't it, Allen. As persons we have to meet so many situations—

TATE: Yes.

RANSOM: —and I want to know if we can't meet them poetically sometimes?

TATE: Well, that's a question.

ELLIOTT: Well, Johnny has raised a question here—a very deep issue which he said he wanted to explore: whether or not we did quit too soon as poets; whether there was something that would go on. Actually, the answer to that, in considerable measures, I have found—more than I realized when I came down here—is that we are going on in varying ways: that Allen is developing an entirely new line—

DAVIDSON: I don't understand John's saying that we quit too soon. We didn't.

ELLIOTT: Well, now wait a minute on this point. And Red has certainly gone on in a tremendously powerful way. Merrill is reaching out into a new dimension that he had not thought was possible for him and gave some proof of it. Certainly, there's no question about Andrew's going on, though he's doing it in novels now.

MOORE: And one more question, apropos of John's parable: is it not true, or is it true or false, or black or white, or gray

—light gray or dark gray—that a Yeats had a choice of being a primary man or a creative man, or a contemplative man; and do not all the Fugitives, each one individually, have the choice at any given point in their life to remain with poetry or go into politics or even combine them both?

RANSOM: Well, Yeats said a very fine thing on that. I don't know the system of Yeats. I've looked at it, and I've read so many synopses of it; and it's so artificial and cumbrous that I think it's no good as a whole. But I think the powerful thing in his conception was of the mask, which is the antithetical man opposed to the primary man, or the antithetical man opposed to the natural man—whether he was primary or contemplative—and he remarked that the value of that as he saw it might be very great for young poets; that he conceived that poets died if they stuck to their natural self, and that all life in a literary man consisted in his playing between the antithetical man and the natural man.

TATE: Great insight, you know.

RANSOM: And I think that probably is very true; or, at any rate, that statement would work in our judgment—

TATE: Well, as a matter of fact, just how does politics appear in Yeats' poetry? It's always elegiac—

RANSOM: [*at the same time*] Well, as you say, it's very limited—

TATE: It's always elegiac, and back of it is the recurrent myth, the Golden Age, the Magnus Annus. It's always back of it. His "romantic Ireland's dead and gone, It's with O'Leary in the grave." It's always the elegiac note.

RANSOM: No, it isn't always—

ELLIOTT: [*at the same time*] No, it's prophetic, too.

RANSOM: —because you've got "Easter, 1916."

ELLIOTT: Oh, well, there are lots of other things. Let's not

bury ourselves in Yeats. I claim a privilege for saying that—
the point I made and tried to leave: Yeats was a mystic; he
couldn't help being a mystic, and his approach to poetry was
couched in these terms. He did want heroes.

RANSOM: [*at the same time*] Yes, but that's a poor disposition
of him—

ELLIOTT: [*at the same time*] Right. I mean, I'm trying to get
at the point you made about the mask and the antithetical
—I forget the exact terms that Yeats himself used. But this
was the thing that Yeats was trying to do; he was trying to
find a vehicle for heroes and for heroic life in modern times.
He was doing what I am trying to do today, and I have not
talked about it here: I am trying to get a "Roundtable of
the Republic" to make some head against this mass attitude
—to select the best in our society, to get an elite for a model
once back into being—which, it seems to me, is the point
towards which Fugitives would naturally head as a problem.
I believe in the other qualities of openness to talents, but I
don't believe in this dragging business. And it seems to me
that a poet who is under the grip of this compulsion is
bound to try to translate it in some form into what he's
doing. I think we've been unaware of it, in some cases; but
Yeats in that insight betrayed what I think was the keynote
in his life, and one that he never found: he became a "stray,
beating his wings," as I have said in this other poem, *Critica
Poetica*, "in air too thin," because he found no understanding of the times into which he could get this vehicle. The
social milieu in which he operated didn't give him this—

BROOKS: I couldn't disagree with you more. It seems to me
that Yeats did what the poet has got to do: tell the truth.
And—

ELLIOTT: Well, who's contested this? This was his truth.
And there are very many—

BROOKS: Yes—

DAVIDSON: I don't see why we always have to talk in terms of William Butler Yeats. [*laughter*]

ELLIOTT: Yes. Let's bury Yeats for the time.

THORP: Could I ask a historical question here, Cleanth?

BROOKS: I wish you would, please.

THORP: This may be in the record somewhere, but I'm not sure that it is. What was the genesis of *I'll Take My Stand?* Were there any of the Fugitives who did not want to come in, in the writing of that book? Were there divisions in the group about it?

TATE: Well, Don would—

THORP: Was there a political-social stage in there between the dissolution of the group and—

TATE: Well, John wrote an introduction, you see. That is, it was a sort of—

MOORE: Manifesto.

TATE: —manifesto, and people more or less had to subscribe to it and feel comfortable—

RANSOM: We had no enabling act. Anyone who wanted—It was free. It was just a new organization. We somehow knew better than to revive it as a move of the Fugitives, because the group would not—

THORP: Well, I re-read most of *I'll Take My Stand* on the train coming down, and I was struck with the amount of concealed research there. Evidently a great deal of thinking had been going on about social matters; at that particular time, of course, in the late 1920's, it would be natural enough for anybody in America. But there are references that seem to conceal a great deal of reading and a great deal of thinking, now, over in this other area. Was that done in the group?

TATE: Don, didn't we—? It was about 1927 that we decided we were going to do the book, and three years elapsed before we got it out.

DAVIDSON: Well, it would be hard to pick the exact date.

TATE: Yes.

DAVIDSON: But if you had to pick a date, I think you'd pick 1925, when the Dayton trial set everything aflame.

ELLIOTT: The Dayton trial was going on when I came back here from Oxford, because—in the summer of 1922, if I remember—

DAVIDSON: No, 1925.

ELLIOTT: Or 1923.

DAVIDSON: 1925.

COWAN: '25.

TATE: It was '25, Bill.

DAVIDSON: 1925.

ELLIOTT: I was here for some reason during that summer—

TATE: It was 1925.

ELLIOTT: —and I thought I could date it from that time—

DAVIDSON: No, it's 1925. The Dayton Trial, and that started a boiling controversy, and started a reconsideration—

ELLIOTT: [*at the same time*] I was here. I headed for Harvard that year.

DAVIDSON: —but it wasn't the only thing that started that reconsideration; but that was just one thing that focused it. Willard is right: there was a lot of reading and maybe some research and a tremendous amount of discussion and correspondence that went on before we ever decided that we would try to get out a symposium. And, as I recall, we made up some possible lists of people that might be solicited as contributors. As John intimated there, we knew better than to ask some to come in, that might have been eligible, because we knew there wouldn't be a close enough agreement to have a central body of principles. And some we sounded out, like Stringfellow Barr, only to discover that he wasn't thinking in the same direction. He said, as I remember, that if we were going to engage in some philosophical discussions on Unamuno or somebody like that, he would be all for it; but if we were going to come down to anything specific, well then he didn't want to take part, because his mind was set in another direction.

RUBIN: Mr. Davidson, why wasn't John Peale Bishop—I know you discussed asking John Peale Bishop to take part in it and I was just curious why—

DAVIDSON: I wasn't very keenly aware of the existence of John Peale Bishop at that time.

LYTLE: He was in France, wasn't he?

TATE: Yes. As I remember—

RUBIN: But in your little article, *"I'll Take My Stand,* A History"—

DAVIDSON: Yes.

RUBIN: —you mention in there, as I recall—

DAVIDSON: Well, it may have been brought up by Allen or somebody—

TATE: I can recall the circumstances, I think; I'm not quite clear about them after so many years. But John Bishop wrote an essay called "The South and Tradition" which he gave at that writers' conference in Charlottesville, in 1931.

DAVIDSON: That was after publication.

TATE: Yes. And after that time, I remember Red and I talked to him a little bit in—

WARREN: Paris.

TATE: —Paris. And I think it was the fact that Red and I were in Paris at that time—I'd known John for some years —that made him conscious of himself again as a Southerner. And he began to think more and more in our direction, but after *I'll Take My Stand;* in fact, I think it had some influence on him.

WARREN: He began to write Southern fiction.

TATE: Southern fiction was going on, but I suppose it didn't occur to him that a statement about Southern culture, our symposium, was possible, really—possible to do anything about.

RANSOM: Wouldn't it be fair to say that the *I'll Take My Stand* group began precisely in the way that the old Fugitive group had begun—with discussions—

DAVIDSON: That's right, that's right. We had Frank Owsley, for instance, that we formed ties with.

RANSOM: —long before there was a policy? And we had two strong members of our faculty, Frank Owsley—the best economic Southern historian that we have ever had—and we had another very powerful man here, Lyle Lanier.*

TATE: Yes.

RANSOM: And we had Jimmy Waller,** the son of an old trustee living just off the campus, who had a big home that was always at our disposal to meet in and even to entertain traveling—

DAVIDSON: That was later; I'll have to correct you there, John. We didn't consort with Jimmy Waller until—

RANSOM: Later.

* A professor in the Psychology Department.
** James A., one of the contributors to *Who Owns America?*

DAVIDSON: —after *Who Owns America?*

RANSOM: Yes.

TATE: That's right.

WARREN: That's right.

RANSOM: I stand corrected.

TATE: Now. I wasn't here during the meetings preceding *I'll Take My Stand.* I was in New York and Paris.

RANSOM: Yes, yes.

TATE: But we corresponded a lot about it.

OWSLEY: May I interject a statement there? Waller came in when we were working on *Who Owns America?*—

TATE: Yes.

OWSLEY: —although we had been consorting with him and his group before that time. But I mean he did write for that.

DAVIDSON: His group didn't get to work, Frank, until 1930, when the crash came; that was what drove them into consultation.

OWSLEY: Yes.

ELLIOTT: Well, just as a footnote to this: I date my relationship to this by the fact that I was coming back from California going to Harvard. It must have been in the summer of 1925 that this happened, and I sat in on some of the peripheral discussions of the thing and was asked, by somebody or other, if I would like to contribute an essay to this—

DAVIDSON: But in 1925 we had no idea of contributing, Bill. It would be the Fugitives.

ELLIOTT: I know, but afterwards somebody wrote me—

DAVIDSON: Yes, yes.

ELLIOTT: —about this as a result and outcome; and at that

time I raised a point which was a point of divergence. With your main preoccupations to get back the values of the South I'm entirely in agreement, and to get the kind of life in America that can control the thing that we are dealing with. But power, in my judgment, is associated with the factors of power. And as a student who has spent his life studying people like Gandhi and the servile state that overwhelmed Agar, another member of this group, and people of that sort—Belloc, Chesterton—I can't feel that the Agrarian thing, stated in the terms you've done it, is capable of giving you the ingredients of the civilization that we have to grapple with.

BROOKS: May I break in just at this point, because our time is running out. I take it that probably it's the sense of this group that we won't spend too much time talking about whether the remedy was feasible or not—

ELLIOTT: Yes. Well, this is the point that I am trying to make at this particular moment, if you will forgive me.

TATE: From the very beginning I thought of the Agrarian group as being rather like the French Encyclopedists. We issued certain ideas, reaffirmed the Southern tradition or standards. Well, the Encyclopedists turned out to be, according to the way you look at it, a great success. They brought on a revolution, or at least they provided the ideas for the revolution. And the Agrarian ideas didn't have such success. I think that's about all you can say about it.

RANSOM: I would hope that we could get in this panel some remarks by Frank Owsley—

ELLIOTT: Owsley, yes.

RANSOM: —who was a member of the panel, and, I think, one of the best heads on the panel.

OWSLEY: Thank you very much for the compliment. I, not being a poet, have remained exceedingly quiet, I think. But since we have come up to the Agrarian Movement, I would like to make some remarks, if you don't object. In the first place, I think this was a revolt against something and a revolt for something. Many of us had been working in different fields of human activity. I had been doing research work in history for a number of years. Although having been a very close personal friend of most of the Fugitives, having been one of the first subscribers to the magazine, having almost a complete set and intending to sell it—of course, selling my friends down the river—during the Second World War because I needed the money, only to find that some graduate student in English had found the set and sold it first. Well, anyway, I did keep up with them as friends, and all this time I was working in history, working in Southern and in sectional history, and more and more aware, both as an individual as well as a member of a group of friends, at least, that the people of America were losing the basic values of civilization, that we were going as a nation into materialism, that money value had become the real basic value, that the sense of community was disappearing, that the common courtesies of life were disappearing—particularly in the North where I went to school as a younger fellow—that you went into a store and were insulted rather than welcomed, that the whole civilization in this country was becoming cruder and cruder, that the things that we thought a civilized country stood for were disappearing. You know the old phraseology in those days was "revolt against the Philistines"—really a revolt against crudeness and rudeness, against those who favored gadgets, and things that concerned everyday conveniences. We looked around and there was another force, I think—in my particular thinking—that did come in. I had been making, and am still making, a study of the causes of the American Civil War. And during the late 1920's and the early 1930's—because, after all, we did continue to write a long time after *I'll Take My Stand;* that was sort of an opener. We didn't propose so much there as we merely affirmed, I think, a set of values. At least I was very much aware of a crusade being levelled against the South, based on poor information, or bad reporting; one of the strangest combinations in all the history of all civilizations—of the Communists and the extreme conservatives speaking the same language. I got hold of a great deal of Communist literature at that time, or rather their propaganda. And it carried a pattern, taking advantage of all of the sectional prejudices; and it was solidly anti-Southern, solidly against the values that we all down in this part of the world had some respect for. So the neo-Confederate angle crept in there, because I think we all had the same feeling, that not only were we trying to reassert values that we thought were basic, but values that also had a considerable bit of a sectional nature. That is, the attack was sectional. And this was, in a way, not just a defense; if it was, it was one of Robert E. Lee's defenses—it was an offensive defense. We became, I think, in our writings very deliberately provocative. I certainly did, and I have been confronted with it from that time till now by the purists in my profession. In fact, there was a book written last year about Southerners writing history in which I was spoken of as a "modern fire-eater." And that did not help my professional standing at all. And in teaching at Columbia University the last two summers, I was confronted with people who said, "You don't look like a fire-eater; you don't even talk like one."

TATE: Why, Frank, I'm surprised.

WARREN: Maybe you're slipping. [*laughter*]

OWSLEY: Well, anyway, the turn of the Old South was simply the seeking of—shall I say?—an example in which at least many of these qualities that we thought were the basic qualities of a civilization were embodied. We advocated, I suppose, an agrarian way of life as at least being the only examples in history where civilization had developed. And also a belief that the high-powered modern industrialization and materialism would not either develop or maintain a civilization very long. Now, of course, I think, as a matter of fact, that agrarianism was a means to an end; and I'm sure that we were not enough economists, then or now—nor was anyone else—to fathom the mysteries of the way of life in terms of economics that will carry on those basic values. We can only look at examples and see what has been done. Summing up briefly, then, I think our revolt was against materialism—the same thing, in a way, that the Fugitives had revolted against—and against stereotyped forms of living and thinking. But it was a revolt to something, and it might not have been the right thing, but at least it was in the right direction, perhaps. That's all I have to say, especially.

BROOKS: Willard, because you originally raised the question, did you have something further in mind, or does this take care of what you wanted to—

THORP: I think so, pretty well. I gather that some people were not asked to contribute, because it was thought they wouldn't go along; and that new individuals were brought into the group. There are some questions about the book itself I'd like to ask, but I don't think they'd be pertinent right now. I'd like to ask Allen what he meant in his essay on Southern religion by saying that feudal society did not produce a feudal religion; but I'll ask him that privately. [*laughter*] There's just one little thing. I noticed in the symposium in the *Shenandoah* some in the group thought that the word ultimately used—"Agrarian," for the movement—was not the right word. Anybody want to comment on that?

TATE: Well, I feel that it wasn't.

OWSLEY: I'd like to say that I think it was a mistake, because by the use of the word "Agrarian" we got tagged, and everybody thought we ought to go out and plow. And this was a philosophy, not an economy.

TATE: I thought it was religious humanism; that was my label for it.

BROOKS: I remember—I think at Oxford; Red says he can't remember it, but I remember distinctly—that Red was objecting to the title of the book and saying it ought to be called *Tracts Against Communism*.

TATE: Yes, I remember Red and I used to talk about that.

RANSOM: Can you take one more comment? I don't want to push this. Well, we have had a certain revival. The book was reprinted, and even the conservative politicians—and certainly the conservative historians—remarked it a good deal. And Clinton Rossiter at Cornell—I'm sure that Mr. Owsley knows him—he made a speech at my college and called on me and said it was very important because he was getting out a book and he had several pages on the Agrarians. And he wanted to know what sort of economy we represented, or what sort of view of the Republic we represented. I said decidedly the Jeffersonian. He was very much relieved at that, because we had been charged with being Fascist—notably by Sherwood Anderson.

TATE: Disciples of Calhoun.

RANSOM: Yes. And I myself have always felt that one of the most hurtful things in our society has been the way that many people have had, mostly ladies, of saying, "My grandfather had a hundred slaves." Another would top that: "Mine had five hundred." And some even went to a thousand. [*laughter*] That's a myth which I think Dr. Owsley has laid in the shade, at least so far as this part of the world is concerned.

OWSLEY: All you have to do is just pull the unpublished census—you ought to watch their faces fall. Those who "had five hundred slaves" suddenly change the subject. [*laughter*]

RANSOM: I think that has been one of the carry-overs of slavery which is most unbecoming—

OWSLEY: That's the moonlight and magnolia—

RANSOM: —and has deeply affected the social pages of our papers in the South.

BROOK: Red, were you trying to get the microphone?

WARREN: Well, I'm not trying very hard. I'm torn by a desire to hear what's being said and a desire to express myself. And I don't know which is going to win.

BROOKS: Let's hear you express yourself.

WARREN: Willard's question sort of jelled out something for me, of how it began. I can't speak in terms of an objective record. I can only speak of what it signified for me— what Agrarianism signified for me. And of late years I have tried to give it some thought, and I must confess that my mind tended to shut up on the subject for about ten years. It seemed irrelevant at one stage to what I was thinking and feeling, except in a sentimental way—I mean at the level of what these things signify; I ceased to think about it during the war years. Before we got in the last war, just before it and several years after, there was the period of unmasking of blank power everywhere. And you felt that all your work was irrelevant to this unmasking of this brute force in the world—that the de-humanizing forces had won. And you had no more relevance in such discussions as we used to have, or are having this morning, except a sort of quarreling with people over the third highball. Well, as I remember the thing as it came to me, there were several appeals in it. It hit me at an age when I was first away from this part of the country for any period of time, having lived in California two years, and a year in New Haven in the Yale Graduate School, and then in Oxford. And I had broken out of the kind of life I was accustomed to in that part of the world I knew. And there was a sentimental appeal for me in this. It happened to coincide with my first attempt, my first story about Southern life—a novelette which I was writing at that time at Oxford. And it had coincided, a little earler that is, with a book on John Brown. But this book led to fiction—that's what the Brown was: a step toward fiction. It was a sentimental appeal and an attempt to re-live something—to recapture, to reassess. This was not thought out; it was just what happened in a sort of an in-stinctive way. And that tied in with some perfectly explicit speculations, in conversation with friends, such as Cleanth at Oxford—and, I must say, this topic would never appeal very much to anybody in California. But the question of— well, there are two questions: one, the sense of the disin-tegration of the notion of the individual in that society we're living in—it's a common notion, we all know—and the relation of that to democracy. It's the machine of power in this so-called democratic state; the machines disintegrate individuals, so you have no individual sense of responsi-bility and no awareness that the individual has a past and a place. He's simply the voting machine; he's everything you pull the lever on if there's any voting at all. And that no-tion got fused with your own personal sentiments and sen-timentalities and your personal pieties and your images of place and people that belong to your own earlier life. And the Confederate element was a pious element, or a great story—a heroic story—a parade of personalities who are also images for these individual values. They were images for it for me, I'm sure, rather than images for a theory of society which had belonged to the South before the war. They became images for that only because they are lost. There was a pretty tough practical guide involved in that; they were out to make power, and money interested them. They can only become images for this other thing in so far as they could not participate later on in their version of a gilded age, probably. I'm not being simple; I mean this is an overstatement that I'm making. There were some correc-tives in Southern society as a matter of preventing that—the excesses of the 70's, 80's and 90's, and so forth, and some that we enjoy now, perhaps. But as to how these elements related in their personal appeal to me? Now, I don't know how much that situation would be shared by others; but I was no economist and didn't fancy myself as one. But for me it was a protest—echoing Frank here—against certain things: against a kind of de-humanizing and disintegrative effect on your notion of what an individual person could be in the sense of a loss of your role in society. You would take it a loss that you had no place in that world. Well, later on I began to read people like Bertrand Russell, during that time—about their idea of how the individual was affected by the state: in the power state he lost existence, disappeared, was a cipher. All of that was involved. And your simpler world is something I think is always necessary—not a golden age, but the past imaginatively conceived and historically conceived in the strictest readings of the researchers. The past is always a rebuke to the present; it's bound to be, one way or another: it's your great rebuke. It's a better rebuke than any dream of the future. It's a better rebuke because you can see what some of the costs were, what frail virtues were achieved in the past by frail men. And it's there, and you can see it, and see what it cost them, and how they had to go at it. And that is a much better rebuke than any dream of a golden age to come, because historians will correct, and imagination will correct, any notion of a simplistic and—well—childish notion of a golden age. The drama of the past that corrects us is the drama of our struggles to be human, or our struggles to define the values of our forebears in the face of their difficulties.

BETHURUM: It's also encouragement.

WARREN: It's encouragement.

BETHURUM: But the thing that impresses me is that I can't see that it isn't always possible in any period under any circumstances to live the life of aristocratic humanism. I feel very strongly all these things, but I think that the Agrarian movement was too pessimistic, was too unhappy about the future.

MOORE: Miss Bethurum, I'd use the word *regressive* as opposed to continuing progress in the world of so-called reality today.

TATE: I don't think it was pessimistic, Dorothy.

BETHURUM: Yes.

DAVIDSON: Oh no, it wasn't pessimistic at all. Pardon me, Dorothy, that's just nonsense.

TATE: [*at the same time*] That was a polemical convention—

DAVIDSON: And Bill has already told you that what you desire—that the aristocratic humanism can prevail in any age—that that is not true, because he's dealing with a power state.

BETHURUM: Yes.

DAVIDSON: And if the power state triumphs, it just can't be.

BETHURUM: [*amidst confusion*] I don't think that; I don't think that.

ELLIOTT: [*at the same time*] Oh, hold on. Now this is a matter on which I claim some competence—

DAVIDSON: Yes. Well, wait a minute; let me get through with my statement, please.

ELLIOTT: Yes, but I didn't tell you that.

DAVIDSON: Well, you implied it.

ELLIOTT: No, I didn't at all imply it.

DAVIDSON: Well, then I misunderstood you.

ELLIOTT: Yes. All right.

DAVIDSON: But anybody that engages in public affairs and

tries to get something done that is outside the movement of the tide, that is either outside it or contrary to it, immediately encounters everything that Red has been discussing, and I can enumerate the specific ways in which people are tied up so that they are either afraid to do anything, or cannot. And it's totally impossible for them to be aristocratic humanists or anything, often, but mere functions of the machine that's going on. Now that's what we were concerned with; and if you don't realize that that is true, you are living in a dream world.

BETHURUM: I have taken part in politics, too, in a small way, and I agree with everything you say. But there never were very many people in any culture—it seems to me—who realized the values we are talking about. There are not very many now.

BROOKS: I think that Red has something to say.

TATE: Dorothy, as a medievalist how can you say that?

BETHURUM: I say it strongly as a medievalist—

RANSOM: Issue of fact.

BETHURUM: —strongly as a medievalist, Allen.

TATE: Well, I want to say this. Please excuse me, Dorothy.

BETHURUM: Yes.

TATE: I'm a little surprised that people didn't applaud Red's speech. I think it was one of the best things we've heard; and he stated my own feelings about it much better than I could. They were just exactly the way I felt about the whole thing, when we began it. It never seemed to me to be a political program, but as a reaffirmation of what Dorothy calls "aristocratic Aristotelianism."

BROOKS: That's why I would like to have Red finish his speech, because I think he may clear up something for us here, and something further—

ELLIOTT: Let's let him do it.

TATE: That is, it was a great mixture of motives we had.

DAVIDSON: I would like to comment on what Allen just said there just briefly. I remind you that in the famous meeting—which the public doesn't know about—that we had with Seward Collins down at Guntersville, that we spent a good part of the time trying to persuade him to publish our poems along with other things—don't you remember?—

TATE: Yes.

DAVIDSON: —poetry and criticism, and succeeded. Once he got away we couldn't control him, but we did do a little of it. That's just by way of saying that the things were all together, really.

BROOKS: Yes, yes.

WARREN: I'm much concerned about the use of the word *aristocratic* in this connection. I think it's a word that's been applied to this group in a—

TATE: Pejorative sense.

WARREN: —sense that I think everybody here would repudiate. I'm not talking about Dorothy's use of it, now. I'm talking about other uses outside, as special kinds of hankerings, you see. And my conception of what we were about was something quite different: I thought we were trying to find—in so far as we were being political—a rational basis for a democracy. That, I thought, was what we were up to.

OWSLEY: I agree with that.

TATE: Yes, I do too.

WARREN: And not to try to enter into competition of whether it was five slaves or five hundred slaves. In fact, that question was relevant only as an image—which Faulkner has now made available even to Frenchmen—for something else, for the crime against the human that we were expiating in our history. And I think that the word *aristocratic* used in a Jeffersonian sense is fine; but that was my notion—that aspect of it at that time. We were trying to find a notion of democracy which would make it possible for people to be people and not to be bosses, or exploiters, or anything else of other people, but to have a community of people, rather than a community of something else. And Bill Elliott years ago, I mean at Oxford, was I think the first person who ever called my attention—when I first met him, our first meeting in a college there; which one it was I forget; Balliol, I guess it was—

ELLIOTT: Balliol.

WARREN: —it was your place; where you were staying that time you were on a visit. Well, anyway, he used to say that the great problem of democracy is a problem of responsible leadership. And he developed that and went on to the question of the role of the individual. I remember the conversation distinctly. And that was in no relation to Agrarianism; but this thing, to me, started something that tied right into that when we began to talk about and write about the Agrarians.

LYTLE: Bill, the thing that you mentioned; I, at the time, as young as I was, was perfectly aware of the problem; how could you have a simple agrarian society—I agree with Red that my feelings were pretty close to that—when you've got these great power states and armies? If you destroyed the industrial set-up, then we would be slaves. But at the same time, I remember in writing "The Hind Tit" I knew then that it was a kind of, say, ideal or romantic version of what the plain farmer—the yeoman farmer—was; but I was making the point deliberately, as a kind of a literary exercise: that such a man basically, if you distributed him sufficiently over the state, would have a definite effect—

would have a slowing-down process on the growth of the central power. And this would come by fixing people in the place where they were responsible citizens because they owned something and could vote. And out of that it seemed to me that I had had some sense of what Frank has since proved: that that really was the basis—finally and ultimately —of what any part of American society was; that any aristocracy we had was certainly a homespun aristocracy. By what it had inherited, you could go from yeomanry, say, into the plantation system in one generation, and take a plain man who has manners and make him a gentleman; but there was not a great difference in that. It was just a different kind of manner.

WARREN: But everybody had manners.

LYTLE: Everybody had manners. [*general conversation*] Manners is the only thing that stands between you and the brute facts of the world.

ELLIOTT: As a Balliol man I yield to the dictum, "Manners maketh man." But let me just correct another point in the record which is relevant, I think, to our discussion and ties right on to what you are saying. Don has felt that I had some feeling that there was an impossibility of any leadership—what people have called in various ways "aristocratic virtues" in a democratic society—because power was the essence of the modern state. Now, I would beg you to think about that a little bit, because power is the essence of any state today. And it has always been the essence of a state. And the point is how you can master power, how can the leaders—Red and I talked about that at Oxford in 1929 or '30, whenever it was—be capable of mastering this beast, of riding the great beast that Plato talked about before Hamilton did?

MOORE: May I speak just one minute, William?

ELLIOTT: All right. But I would like to finish this remark. Lasky perverted Lord Acton, in his usual way, by misquoting him. He said that Acton had said, "All power corrupts, and absolute power corrupts absolutely." Acton actually said, "Power tends to corrupt" (there can be no doubt about that) and then that "absolute power corrupts absolutely" (and this is correct). What we were concerned with as a group was to find—out of that revolt which Penn Warren has described more accurately, I think, than anybody in terms of its feelings—how to reaffirm those things that could control power by getting control of the men who could get power. But if we did not get people who could get power, Don, we would lose the battle just as infallibly as anything in the world. Therefore, it was important for the poet, if he could, to get hold of the motives that people live by and to get the values reaffirmed in the people who were in power. This is our whole problem as a nation today. And it isn't a lost cause by any manner of means, though it's a very difficult cause. And if we don't understand the motive forces of power—Johnny and I used to talk about this thing, that he put so aptly, about the New Deal and its continuation, about change as the profit of the modern state. He, I think, did me the justice to say he had come to the conclusion that the books I had written were more nearly on the track in trying to get a balance once more between power and the things that motivate and control the men who take power. This is the point that I think as poets we are bound to be concerned with in our times: but how can we do that? And I don't think it can be done, Don, just by crying out.

WARREN: Last night, Charlie Moss * and I were talking, after you all had left his house. He said, talking about Agrarianism, "The question of civilizing and making progress amounts to a moral progress, or civilizing progress, and is a matter always of a fifth column in a society." And the effect is slow; if we had any function, we were a fifth column. We couldn't step out and take over the powers of the state. Poetry is a fifth column—

* Executive Editor of the *Nashville Banner;* Vanderbilt '24.

ELLIOTT: That's right.

WARREN: —in the same way. Universities should be fifth columns, but they usually aren't.

ELLIOTT: You have to educate your masters—

MOORE: Just to to get the record clear, I agree with Brother Elliott that the problem today is power in politics; but I want to make it clear that in my humble opinion the so-called "Fugitives" refer to the period of 1922 to 1925 and relate primarily to pure poetry—if there is such a thing, and George Moore tried to prove there was. I believe that we are now far beyond the Fugitive period which, from the librarian's point of view, is definitive and limited. And, as Mr. Ransom said, when he was writing for *The Fugitive* he was not thinking about public affairs. And very few of us were, but if some were I'd like to hear about it. And that clearly it's indicated that there is a need for a second re-union—possibly next year and possibly under some auspices that might be friendly to the cause—to have a meeting on the Agrarian issue which is certainly vital and important. And, third, can there be some action made by this group concerning the manuscripts which Davidson has guarded, and which should be made available to selected scholars and not molding or lost as might be the case. There's a lot of important material that ought to be deposited in the Library and made available along the lines that we have seen Mrs. Cowan utilize. And there are others who want to do that. And the more it can be done fully and with full disclosure, the better it will be for defining the origins and development of the Fugitive group and the later group that followed it, which seems most important to me. And last I'd like to say that I had a long talk with Alfred Starr last night, and he asked to tell you that he had to go away today. He's going to the Opera in Atlanta to see Puccini performed, and he regrets not being here but wishes to express his most cordial welcome and temporary farewell in that cause. He particularly asked me to tell Don that he regretted it was not Wagner, but he would try to make do with Puccini. [*laughter*]

COWAN: May I say one sentence that may not—

BROOKS: Yes, Mrs. Cowan.

COWAN: —you gentlemen may not consider relevant. But, for whatever it's worth, the four men—the four Fugitives— who became men of letters in the sense that they gave— they risked—their lives on literature—poetry became not a sideline with them, but a primary pursuit—those were the four who went on with Agrarianism. And that has seemed to me relevant.

RUBIN: It certainly is relevant.

BROOKS: Well, I think that as far as the record is concerned, it's well stamped down in the record, it's perfectly clear that the line is drawn. I think maybe that's just as well. It does seem to me—I'm exceeding my role as titular moderator here to say—that if one makes two or three fairly simple distinctions, I don't think that there is any basic argument here. I don't think that we ever judge the worth of a poem by its success as a remedy. On the other hand, a good diagnosis is always the basis of any remedy. The poet is bound to be concerned, ultimately, with the good life and with the nature of reality. And I think it's terribly interesting to find out about the historical problem of composition and theories of composition, particularly as held by various people, but it seems to me that you can have all sorts of theories of composition and still have your big problem of evaluating the poem, as documents giving you a certain kind of truth.

A SUMMING UP

Saturday Noon, May 5

By CLEANTH BROOKS

And now I have a few words to say, and though I speak from an excited mind and out of a full heart, I will try to be modest in scope. As a matter of fact, if there were a different kind of audience for whom I were summing up, there would be some point in a detailed summary. But I shall discard any notions that I had of that kind. That very fine though limited poet, and good provincial, and representative man of the eighteenth century, Dr. Samuel Johnson, used to be very proud of his college at Oxford—Pembroke College—because he said, it was a "nest of singing birds." There had been lots of poets there. He was able to count up three or four. As a matter of fact, Johnson's phrase describes exactly the present occasion, which has been so pleasant to all of us. We have been looking at a last year's bird nest—a rather glorious bird's nest. [*laughter*] A bird's nest of considerable more splendor than the rather modest little nest—it was no more than that, I'm afraid when all is said and done—that Dr. Johnson, with a fine sanity and proper piety, rejoiced in.

What does one examine a bird's nest for, particularly when a good many of the birds have flown? And even the birds that remain in this habitat are no longer fledglings—I am looking at that fine poet, Donald Davidson, who spreads his own wings and beats the air powerfully. But many have flown, migratory

219

birds. I suppose in one sense the study of bird-nest building could be regarded as an art—as the study of the kind of community out of which literature grows. Dr. Samuel Johnson would have called—in fact, did call it—the art of nidification, bird-nest building. I suppose we have learned a great deal about the context out of which this brilliant group came. I, certainly, have learned a great deal; because the campfires were still glowing when I was here as a freshman, and one went on from one to the other, and the embers were not yet quite cold. The Fugitives were getting ready to suspend, but by a series of lucky accidents I ran into Red, and then through him met Andrew; as a matter of fact, those meetings changed very quickly my notion of the glamorous life—which was originally that of being a really shifty halfback—to authorship. Here were people who actually wrote poems and stories and got them printed. That redirection of interest came for me earlier than the meeting with Donald and with John in classes a little later.

I have learned—I'm sure all of us have learned—a great deal about this community. I hadn't realized, for example—and it's been exhilarating to realize—how powerful some of the tensions were in the group, and how useful they must have been—the pull back and forth. I won't call them "divisions"; I'll call them tensions. I hadn't realized—I couldn't realize—the role that Sidney Hirsch must have played, for example. Or all sorts of other things. But all that is, let's hope, in the tape. And I'm not going to try to summarize that part or talk about it. As far as history—literary history—is concerned, it's there embalmed in a manner of speaking; and somebody, the scholar of the future, can work at it. I don't think it'll last any seven centuries; with the way in which the American graduate schools are going into super-production, I am sure that that tape will be worn out in ten years. [*laughter*] What I am really concerned in is this matter: what is the use—aside from history and preserving the past—what's the use of the study of literary bird-nest building? Does anyone have the foolishness to think that thereby he can learn how to build such a nest?

I don't think so. I would use an analogy: I am very much interested in talking about poems and trying to see, in so far as one can see, how they are put together, how they are built. But if you do that, very frequently somebody says, "You are trying to find out the secret so you can write a poem by a formula." That's not the point at all. One doesn't study these things in any hope that they can be reproduced in that fashion.

Yet I think that there is an application to the present and even a pointing toward the future in such study and not merely reference to an antiquarian's past. Because one can learn, I believe, some of the conditions which have to be propitious for the development of a literary community. I think here that that really remarkable book—little read and misunderstood—by T. S. Eliot, called *Notes Toward a Definition of Culture*—is very important. His theme, as you will remember, is that you can't fabricate a civilization as you can a house or a wall; you grow one, or you find it growing. You water it, you nurture it, you cultivate it, you are careful about it; you can do something to promote its growth but you can't create it *ex nihilo*. The burden of what has been said, through the very interesting sessions, seems to me all to bear on that point.

I've been interested in how much classics came into the development of the Fugitives, the study of Latin and Greek; a sense of a community in some very real sense, even with family ties back and forth; the sense of concrete exchange of ideas; the sense of common principles so deep and so common that you didn't even have to talk about them, but they were there underneath you all the time, and you could unconsciously rest upon them; and, therefore, put your attention on the other things. All of those matters I think are terribly important. For me they are much more important now than they would have been for me eight years ago; because I have spent the last eight years at a big Eastern university. And I have learned a great deal to admire in that university. On the other hand, what I have learned there makes me regard this experience as all the more remarkable and precious. Now I am not going to do what I would consider the snide trick of deprecating the university where I now teach in order to glorify this occasion. I think that Yale has some very precious things. It has qualities which Vanderbilt might well aspire to. It has certain other things—resources in books, manuscripts, men, and money—to which Vanderbilt probably cannot aspire. But it lacks, at least unless I am completely prejudiced, this very precious thing which Vanderbilt once had. Does Vanderbilt itself still maintain the cultural conditions which made the emergence of the Fugitive Group possible? I certainly do not know. But the disintegration that is going on all over the country makes me fear that the conditions necessary for the nurture of a literary community such as the Fugitives' was may have disappeared. But the situation of the young writer in all of our more distinguished universities makes me fearful. The young writer has plenty of talent. But his environment in its sophistication is aridifying. The young writers know too much. (Of course, they really don't know too much; you can't know too much if you really know it.) But they do run into the difficulty of knowing all the techniques as abstract techniques, knowing the full bag of tricks as a special bag of tricks; knowing what the newest fad is going to be before the new bandwagon actually rumbles around the corner. I think such knowledge can be a crippling thing. I think that a certain kind of provincialism, a certain kind of innocence—though I think that probably is a wrong term—is indispensable.

In saying these things, I am probably speaking to the converted here. I don't know, of course, how many of you have any real influence over Vanderbilt's destinies. But what I would like to say, in summing up, is this: there is probably nothing that any of us can do to insure the emergence of another group like the Fugitives. Inspection of last year's bird's nest will not tell us how to make Vanderbilt once again a nest of singing birds. The fortunate circumstance of the concurrence of so many talented men is unpredictable and rarely repeated. But there are other important matters about which we might do something. Granted the need for talent, granted a great many other things, unless you have the proper seed bed, the proper nurturing circumstances, the seed of a literary movement perishes. It perishes from adverse conditions, but it can also actually be killed by the wrong sort of kindness, or even by too much kindness—by a "programizing" of the whole thing. Now, this is all that I have to say. Let me express again my own personal, very deep sense of appreciation at being able to be at such a meeting and turn us back to our only begetter, Mr. Randall Stewart. [*applause*]

STEWART: I don't have to say anything, do I? Except that this has been great, and God bless you. [*laughter*]

WARREN: Randall, may I lower the tone of the conversation? [*laughter*]

STEWART: Yes, you certainly may.

WARREN: Not quite to the smoking car level, but a story occurs to me. It's a little indecorous, but we're among friends and all of that. There was a sociological survey made several years ago I saw a news account of: of juvenile delinquency among young girls, girls in New York City. And they had many thousand interviewed, and asked them why they did it. And there were about seven or eight hundred said, "My mother doesn't like me," and about two thousand of them said, "My father doesn't like me"—Merrill probably can give you the proportion of these things—and another seventeen hundred said, "Well, they quarrel at night, and I have to go outdoors to keep from hearing their quarrels," and "I don't like my baby brother," and one thing and another. This got down to four thousand, nine-hundred and ninety-nine of them. And then they had one more little girl to talk to—and they asked her why she did it, and she said, "I likes it." [*laughter*] Well, I think that's what the Rockefeller Foundation's going to find out— [*laughter*] We haven't got any alibis.

Notes on design: *The triskelion at the top of the title page was drawn from a plaque that hangs in the Vanderbilt English Department commemorating the Fugitives; it is a symbol favored by the group in the early 1920's. The text of this book is in 12-point Linotype Baskerville, with larger sizes of Monotype Bulmer italic used for the headings, on the title page, and for stamping the cover. The book was designed by Robert McGaw. It was set, printed, and bound by the Parthenon Press in Nashville, Tennessee.*